I Have, Who Has?

MATH

3–4

Written by

Trisha Callella

Editor: Carla Hamaguchi
Cover Illustrator: Corbin Hillam
Production: Moonhee Pak and Carrie Rickmond
Designer: Moonhee Pak
Art Director: Tom Cochrane

Table of Contents

I HAVE, WHO HAS is a series of books that provide interactive group activities. The activities consist of game cards that students read and interactively answer. Each card game consists of 40 cards. The game starts when a student reads the first card. The student who has the card with the answer reads his or her card. The game continues in this manner until the last card is read. The last card's question "loops" back to the first card.

Introduction

This book provides a fun, interactive way for students to practice various math skills. This resource includes over 35 card games that will improve students' listening skills and teach standards-based skills and strategies. The skills covered include:

- Addition
- Subtraction
- Place Value
- Multiplication
- Division
- Equations
- Fractions
- Number Patterns
- Algebra
- Measurement
- Money
- Time
- Probability
- Area and Perimeter
- Geometry Terms

There is also an active listening and enrichment activity included for most games. This component gives students practice in active listening and extends their learning to the application level.

Even better is the fact that there is hardly any prep work required to start these games in your class. Simply make copies of the game cards, cut them apart, and you are ready to go! These engaging games will keep students entertained as they are learning valuable math skills.

ORGANIZATION

There are 40 reproducible cards for each game. The cards are arranged in columns (top to bottom) in the order they will be read by the class. A reproducible active listening and enrichment page follows every set of game cards. The interactive card games for reviewing skills and strategies can be used alone or in conjunction with this reproducible page to have students practice active listening, increase active participation, provide enrichment, and extend and transfer the learning and accountability of each student.

INSTRUCTIONS FOR I HAVE, WHO HAS GAME CARDS

1) Photocopy two sets of the game cards. (Each game has four pages of 10 cards each.)

2) Cut apart one set of game cards. Mix up the cards. Pass out at least one card to each student. (There are 40 cards to accommodate large class sizes. If your class size is less than 40, then some students will have two cards. The important thing is that every student has at least one card.)

3) Keep one copy of the game cards as your reference to the correct order. The cards are printed in order in columns from top to bottom and left to right.

4) Have the student with the first game card begin the game by saying *I have the first card. Who has . . . ?* As each student reads a card, monitor your copy to make sure students are reading the cards in the correct order. If students correctly matched each card, then the last card read will "loop" back to the first card.

INSTRUCTIONS FOR ACTIVE LISTENING & ENRICHMENT PAGE

1) This page is optional and is not necessary to play the game.

2) Copy one page for each student or pair of students.

3) Make sure each student has a light-colored crayon or highlighter (not a marker or pencil) to color over the correct boxes as read.

4) As each matching card is read, provide time for students to complete the grid or chart at the top of the page. If the game is slow for a particular class, two students can help each other with one reproducible page.

5) Some games require an overhead transparency. For those activities, copy the reproducible on an overhead transparency. Display the transparency as students play the game.

6) Use the answer key on pages 198–204 to check students' answers.

WHAT TO WATCH FOR

1) Students who have difficulty locating the correct boxes on the active listening and enrichment page after the first game (establish familiarity with the format) may have visual discrimination difficulties.

2) Students who have difficulty reading their card at the correct time may have difficulties with attention, hearing, active listening, or the concepts being reinforced.

VARIATIONS

Visual Aids

- For students who are challenged with mental math, pass out one of the following for students to work out the problems: blank paper, dry erase board, or white copy paper slipped into a page protector to be written on with a dry erase marker.
- Have students write the problem they are asking (from their game card) on a dry erase board to hold up while they read their card.
- As each student reads the card, write down what he or she is asking for on an overhead transparency.
- Have students complete the reproducible page with a partner or alone.
- If you are not using the reproducible pages, provide 100 boards for those students challenged by mental math.

Timed Version

1) Follow the instructions to prepare the game cards so that each student has at least one. Play without the reproducible page. Tell students that they will play the game twice. Challenge them to beat their time in the second round.

2) Have students play the same game again the next day. Can they beat their time again? Remember to mix up the cards and redistribute them before each game.

3) The more students play, the better they will understand the concepts covered in each game. They will also develop stronger phrasing and fluency in reading.

Small Groups

1) Photocopy one set of game cards (four pages, 40 cards total) for each small group. Play without the reproducible page.

2) Cut apart the cards, mix them up, and give a set to each group.

3) Have each group play. You can time the groups to encourage them to pay close attention, read quickly, and stay on task. Which group is the fastest?

4) By playing in smaller groups, each student has more cards. This raises the individual accountability, activity, time on task, and reinforcement opportunities per student.

I have the **first card.**

Who has the number that is
2 more than 12?

I have **96.**

Who has the number that is
10 more than 71?

I have **14.**

Who has the number that is
10 more than 67?

I have **81.**

Who has the number that is
9 less than 35?

I have **77.**

Who has the number that is
9 more than 45?

I have **26.**

Who has the number that is
11 more than 50?

I have **54.**

Who has the number that is
11 more than 37?

I have **61.**

Who has the number that is
2 more than 43?

I have **48.**

Who has the number that is
2 less than 98?

I have **45.**

Who has the number that is
10 less than 69?

Number Sense

I have **59.**

Who has the number that is
9 more than 43?

I have **25.**

Who has the number that is
11 more than 58?

I have **52.**

Who has the number that is
11 more than 67?

I have **69.**

Who has the number that is
2 more than 44?

I have **78.**

Who has the number that is
2 less than 91?

I have **46.**

Who has the number that is
10 less than 83?

I have **89.**

Who has the number that is
10 more than 18?

I have **73.**

Who has the number that is
9 more than 55?

I have **28.**

Who has the number that is
9 less than 34?

I have **64.**

Who has the number that is
11 less than 50?

I Have, Who Has? Math • 3–4 © 2006 Creative Teaching Press

Number Sense

I have **39.**

Who has the number that is
2 less than 36?

I have **85.**

Who has the number that is
10 less than 76?

I have **34.**

Who has the number that is
10 more than 33?

I have **66.**

Who has the number that is
9 more than 47?

I have **43.**

Who has the number that is
9 less than 32?

I have **56.**

Who has the number that is
11 less than 53?

I have **23.**

Who has the number that is
11 more than 56?

I have **42.**

Who has the number that is
2 less than 94?

I have **67.**

Who has the number that is
2 more than 83?

I have **92.**

Who has the number that is
10 more than 31?

Number Sense

I have **41.**

Who has the number that is
9 less than 47?

I have **74.**

Who has the number that is
11 less than 86?

I have **38.**

Who has the number that is
11 more than 72?

I have **75.**

Who has the number that is
2 less than 51?

I have **83.**

Who has the number that is
2 more than 61?

I have **49.**

Who has the number that is
10 more than 58?

I have **63.**

Who has the number that is
10 less than 75?

I have **68.**

Who has the number that is
11 more than 76?

I have **65.**

Who has the number that is
9 more than 65?

I have **87.**

Who has the first card?

Number Sense

Directions: As your classmates identify the answers, write each number in the grid from left to right and top to bottom.

Start →									
A	B	C	D	E	F	G	H	I	J

Now use the completed grid above to answer the questions.

1. Look at the last number you wrote in Column A. What is 10 more? _____

2. Look at the first number you wrote in Column F. What is 11 less? _____

3. Look at the last number you wrote in Column H. What is 2 more? _____

4. Look at the first number you wrote in Column J. What is 10 less? _____

5. Look at the last number you wrote in Column E. What is 9 more? _____

6. Look at the first number you wrote in Column C. What is 11 less? _____

7. Look at the last number you wrote in Column B. What is 2 less? _____

8. Look at the first number you wrote in Column I. What is 9 less? _____

9. Look at the last number you wrote in Column G. What is 11 more? _____

10. Look at the first number you wrote in Column D. What is 9 more? _____

11. Look at the last number you wrote in Column F. What is 10 less? _____

12. Look at the first number you wrote in Column E. What is 11 less? _____

I Have, Who Has: Math • 3–4 © 2006 Creative Teaching Press

Number Sense—Making 100

I have the **first card.**

Who has my partner to make 100 if I have 74?

I have **77.**

Who has my partner to make 100 if I have 55?

I have **26.**

Who has my partner to make 100 if I have 51?

I have **45.**

Who has my partner to make 100 if I have 39?

I have **49.**

Who has my partner to make 100 if I have 12?

I have **61.**

Who has my partner to make 100 if I have 11?

I have **88.**

Who has my partner to make 100 if I have 33?

I have **89.**

Who has my partner to make 100 if I have 47?

I have **67.**

Who has my partner to make 100 if I have 23?

I have **53.**

Who has my partner to make 100 if I have 32?

Number Sense—Making 100

I have **68.**

Who has my partner to make
100 if I have 14?

I have **12.**

Who has my partner to make
100 if I have 76?

I have **86.**

Who has my partner to make
100 if I have 75?

I have **24.**

Who has my partner to make
100 if I have 31?

I have **25.**

Who has my partner to make
100 if I have 42?

I have **69.**

Who has my partner to make
100 if I have 87?

I have **58.**

Who has my partner to make
100 if I have 71?

I have **13.**

Who has my partner to make
100 if I have 69?

I have **29.**

Who has my partner to make
100 if I have 88?

I have **31.**

Who has my partner to make
100 if I have 38?

I Have, Who Has?: Math • 3–4 © 2006 Creative Teaching Press

I have **62.**

Who has my partner to make 100 if I have 41?

I have **66.**

Who has my partner to make 100 if I have 68?

I have **59.**

Who has my partner to make 100 if I have 45?

I have **32.**

Who has my partner to make 100 if I have 17?

I have **55.**

Who has my partner to make 100 if I have 86?

I have **83.**

Who has my partner to make 100 if I have 24?

I have **14.**

Who has my partner to make 100 if I have 77?

I have **76.**

Who has my partner to make 100 if I have 81?

I have **23.**

Who has my partner to make 100 if I have 34?

I have **19.**

Who has my partner to make 100 if I have 36?

I have **64.**

Who has my partner to make 100 if I have 27?

I have **40.**

Who has my partner to make 100 if I have 66?

I have **73.**

Who has my partner to make 100 if I have 53?

I have **34.**

Who has my partner to make 100 if I have 29?

I have **47.**

Who has my partner to make 100 if I have 65?

I have **71.**

Who has my partner to make 100 if I have 64?

I have **35.**

Who has my partner to make 100 if I have 83?

I have **36.**

Who has my partner to make 100 if I have 22?

I have **17.**

Who has my partner to make 100 if I have 60?

I have **78.**

Who has the first card?

I Have, Who Has!: Math • 3–4 © 2006 Creative Teaching Press

Number Sense—Making 100

Directions: As your classmates identify the answers, highlight or lightly color the numbers.

1	2	3	4	5	6	7	8	9	10
11	12	13	14	15	16	17	18	19	20
21	22	23	24	25	26	27	28	29	30
31	32	33	34	35	36	37	38	39	40
41	42	43	44	45	46	47	48	49	50
51	52	53	54	55	56	57	58	59	60
61	62	63	64	65	66	67	68	69	70
71	72	73	74	75	76	77	78	79	80
81	82	83	84	85	86	87	88	89	90
91	92	93	94	95	96	97	98	99	100

Choose 15 numbers from the completed grid that you did **not** highlight or color. Write each number and the compatible to make 100 in the chart below.

	+		= 100
	+		= 100
	+		= 100
	+		= 100
	+		= 100
	+		= 100
	+		= 100
	+		= 100
	+		= 100
	+		= 100
	+		= 100
	+		= 100
	+		= 100
	+		= 100
	+		= 100

I have the **first card.**

Who has 80 – 50?

I have **400.**

Who has 540 – 340?

I have **30.**

Who has 150 – 80?

I have **200.**

Who has 190 – 80?

I have **70.**

Who has 1,400 – 800?

I have **110.**

Who has 340 – 280?

I have **600.**

Who has 240 – 60?

I have **60.**

Who has 480 – 430?

I have **180.**

Who has 600 – 200?

I have **50.**

Who has 220 – 180?

I have **40.**

Who has 330 – 100?

I have **310.**

Who has 480 – 360?

I have **230.**

Who has 250 – 40?

I have **120.**

Who has 650 – 430?

I have **210.**

Who has 170 – 80?

I have **220.**

Who has 500 – 240?

I have **90.**

Who has 330 – 230?

I have **260.**

Who has 470 – 40?

I have **100.**

Who has 420 – 110?

I have **430.**

Who has 400 – 40?

I have **360.**

Who has 500 – 250?

I have **350.**

Who has 380 – 220?

I have **250.**

Who has 380 – 140?

I have **160.**

Who has 300 – 150?

I have **240.**

Who has 350 – 210?

I have **150.**

Who has 190 – 60?

I have **140.**

Who has 300 – 130?

I have **130.**

Who has 260 – 240?

I have **170.**

Who has 500 – 150?

I have **20.**

Who has 320 – 310?

Subtraction—Dropping Common Zeros

I have **10.**

Who has 300 – 220?

I have **500.**

Who has 500 – 120?

I have **80.**

Who has 300 – 110?

I have **380.**

Who has 400 – 80?

I have **190.**

Who has 400 – 130?

I have **320.**

Who has 320 – 40?

I have **270.**

Who has 580 – 280?

I have **280.**

Who has 400 – 70?

I have **300.**

Who has 880 – 380?

I have **330.**

Who has the first card?

I Have, Who Has?: Math • 3–4 © 2006 Creative Teaching Press

Subtraction—Dropping Common Zeros

Directions: Complete the maze by highlighting the answers as your classmates identify them.

Start *	330	360	250	240	350	160
30	280	430	470	140	170	150
70	380	260	220	10	20	130
600	180	290	120	80	190	50
700	400	560	310	300	270	390
110	200	90	100	500	460	440
60	550	210	340	380	370	350
50	40	230	480	320	280	**Finish 330**

Use the 16 numbers you skipped in the maze above to fill in the table below. Write each number in any box in the first column. Then write the answer to each subtraction problem. The first one is done for you.

Number from Table				
330	–	120	=	210
	–	100	=	
	–	90	=	
	–	120	=	
	–	130	=	
	–	50	=	
	–	80	=	
	–	120	=	
	–	110	=	
	–	100	=	
	–	40	=	
	–	120	=	
	–	110	=	
	–	70	=	
	–	80	=	
	–	100	=	

I Have, Who Has!: Math • 3–4 © 2006 Creative Teaching Press

Adding from Left to Right

I have the **first card.**

Who has the sum of
35 + 44?

I have **49.**

Who has the sum of
27 + 31?

I have **79.**

Who has the sum of
26 + 13?

I have **58.**

Who has the sum of
73 + 25?

I have **39.**

Who has the sum of
15 + 22?

I have **98.**

Who has the sum of
23 + 45?

I have **37.**

Who has the sum of
61 + 24?

I have **68.**

Who has the sum of
28 + 41?

I have **85.**

Who has the sum of
13 + 36?

I have **69.**

Who has the sum of
51 + 31?

I have **82.**

Who has the sum of
30 + 57?

I have **99.**

Who has the sum of
17 + 11?

I have **87.**

Who has the sum of
22 + 66?

I have **28.**

Who has the sum of
34 + 31?

I have **88.**

Who has the sum of
13 + 25?

I have **65.**

Who has the sum of
24 + 24?

I have **38.**

Who has the sum of
31 + 36?

I have **48.**

Who has the sum of
22 + 37?

I have **67.**

Who has the sum of
84 + 15?

I have **59.**

Who has the sum of
31 + 41?

I Have, Who Has: Math • 3–4 © 2006 Creative Teaching Press

Adding from Left to Right

I have **72.**

Who has the sum of
42 + 12?

I have **81.**

Who has the sum of
12 + 30?

I have **54.**

Who has the sum of
12 + 32?

I have **42.**

Who has the sum of
13 + 30?

I have **44.**

Who has the sum of
23 + 22?

I have **43.**

Who has the sum of
12 + 13?

I have **45.**

Who has the sum of
31 + 44?

I have **25.**

Who has the sum of
25 + 41?

I have **75.**

Who has the sum of
70 + 11?

I have **66.**

Who has the sum of
11 + 30?

 # Adding from Left to Right

I have **41.**

Who has the sum of
12 + 41?

I have **93.**

Who has the sum of
41 + 11?

I have **53.**

Who has the sum of
11 + 50?

I have **52.**

Who has the sum of
31 + 43?

I have **61.**

Who has the sum of
44 + 45?

I have **74.**

Who has the sum of
16 + 30?

I have **89.**

Who has the sum of
40 + 24?

I have **46.**

Who has the sum of
23 + 32?

I have **64.**

Who has the sum of
61 + 32?

I have **55.**

Who has the first card?

I Have, Who Has?: Math • 3–4 © 2006 Creative Teaching Press

Adding from Left to Right

Directions: As your classmates identify the answers, write each number in the correct suitcase.

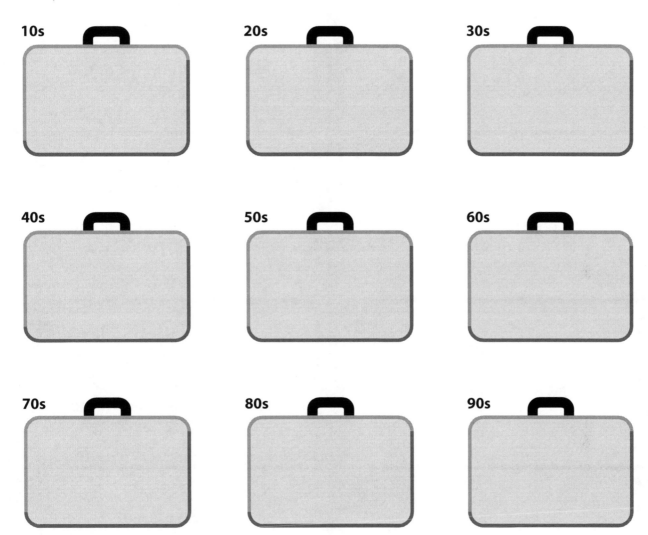

Write two numbers with less than 5 ones from each suitcase to complete each equation. Use the strategy, adding from left to right.

Suitcase of 40s   _____ + _____ = _____

Suitcase of 50s   _____ + _____ = _____

Suitcase of 60s   _____ + _____ = _____

Suitcase of 70s   _____ + _____ = _____

Suitcase of 80s   _____ + _____ = _____

I Have, Who Has?: Math • 3–4 © 2006 Creative Teaching Press

Place Value 1

I have the **first card.**

Who has the value of the
7 in 372?

I have **1 thousand
or 1,000.**

Who has the value of the
5 in 675?

I have **7 tens or 70.**

Who has the value of the
2 in 829?

I have **5 ones or 5.**

Who has the value of the
7 in 7,306?

I have **2 tens or 20.**

Who has the value of the
6 in 196?

I have **7 thousands
or 7,000.**

Who has the value of the
8 in 7,398?

I have **6 ones or 6.**

Who has the value of the
3 in 4,391?

I have **8 ones or 8.**

Who has the value of the
1 in 3,197?

I have **3 hundreds
or 300.**

Who has the value of the
1 in 1,680?

I have **1 hundred or 100.**

Who has the value of the
4 in 9,549?

I Have, Who Has?: Math • 3–4 © 2006 Creative Teaching Press

Place Value 1

I have **4 tens or 40.**

Who has the value of the
2 in 692?

I have **3 ones or 3.**

Who has the value of the
9 in 9,720?

I have **2 ones or 2.**

Who has the value of the
4 in 4,502?

I have **9 thousands
or 9,000.**

Who has the value of the
6 in 561?

I have **4 thousands
or 4,000.**

Who has the value of the
9 in 597?

I have **6 tens or 60.**

Who has the value of the
2 in 4,239?

I have **9 tens or 90.**

Who has the value of the
5 in 9,852?

I have **2 hundreds
or 200.**

Who has the value of the
0 in 3,408?

I have **5 tens or 50.**

Who has the value of the
3 in 473?

I have **0 tens or 0.**

Who has the value of the
4 in 5,394?

Place Value 1

I have **4 ones or 4.**

Who has the value of the
9 in 589?

I have **2 thousands
or 2,000.**

Who has the value of the
6 in 7,611?

I have **9 ones or 9.**

Who has the value of the
3 in 934?

I have **6 hundreds
or 600.**

Who has the value of the
9 in 3,901?

I have **3 tens or 30.**

Who has the value of the
5 in 5,048?

I have **9 hundreds
or 900.**

Who has the value of the
3 in 3,455?

I have **5 thousands
or 5,000.**

Who has the value of the
8 in 6,830?

I have **3 thousands
or 3,000.**

Who has the value of the
4 in 2,477?

I have **8 hundreds
or 800.**

Who has the value of the
2 in 2,399?

I have **4 hundreds
or 400.**

Who has the value of the
8 in 782?

I Have, Who Has?: Math • 3–4 © 2006 Creative Teaching Press

Place Value 1

I have **8 tens or 80.**

Who has the value of the 7 in 732?

I have **6 thousands or 6,000.**

Who has the value of the 1 in 991?

I have **7 hundreds or 700.**

Who has the value of the 8 in 8,331?

I have **1 one or 1.**

Who has the value of the 1 in 9,518?

I have **8 thousands or 8,000.**

Who has the value of the 5 in 9,540?

I have **1 ten or 10.**

Who has the value of the zero in 2,920?

I have **5 hundreds or 500.**

Who has the value of the 7 in 897?

I have **0 ones or 0.**

Who has the smallest whole place value location?

I have **7 ones or 7.**

Who has the value of the 6 in 6,302?

I have the **ones place.**

Who has the first card?

Place Value 1

Directions: Complete the maze by highlighting the answers as your classmates identify them.

6 ones or 6	2 tens or 20	7 tens or 70	**Start** *	8 tens or 80	1 hundred or 100	5 tens or 50
3 hundreds or 300	4 ones or 4	6 hundred	8 thousands or 8,000	3 tens or 30	5 thousands or 5,000	8 hundreds or 800
1 thousand or 1,000	5 ones or 5	9 hundred	2 tens or 20	9 ones or 9	6 ones or 6	2 thousands or 2,000
0 tens or 0	7 thousands or 7,000	3 thousand	0 tens or 0	4 ones or 4	0 tens or 0	6 hundreds or 600
2 tens or 20	8 ones or 8	1 hundred or 100	4 tens or 40	3 ones or 3	2 hundreds or 200	9 hundreds or 900
8 hundred	5 hundred	1 thousand	2 ones or 2	4 thousands or 4,000	6 tens or 60	3 thousands or 3,000
7 tens or 70	3 ones or 3	1 one or 1	6 ones or 6	9 tens or 90	9 thousands or 9,000	4 hundreds or 400
8 tens or 80	0 ones or 0	1 ten or 10	6 thousands or 6,000	5 tens or 50	3 ones or 3	8 tens or 80
5 tens or 50	**Finish** ones place	9 ones or 9	7 ones or 7	5 hundreds or 500	8 thousands or 8,000	7 hundreds or 700

Choose three boxes that are **not** highlighted. Create a four-digit number that includes the given place value.
Example: If the box says "2 tens or 20," you could write 6,5**2**0.

1. _____

2. _____

3. _____

I Have, Who Has?: Math • 3–4 © 2006 Creative Teaching Press

Place Value 2

I have the **first card.**

Who has the value of the
4 in 48,980?

I have **47,602.**

Who has the value of the
6 in 762,119?

I have **4 ten thousands
or 40,000.**

Who has the value of the
8 in 893,400?

I have **6 ten thousands
or 60,000.**

Who has the value of
900,000 + 20,000 + 5,000 + 300 + 60?

I have **8 hundred thousands
or 800,000.**

Who has the value of the
2 in 923,505?

I have **925,360.**

Who has the value of the
3 in 345,000?

I have **2 ten thousands
or 20,000.**

Who has the value of the
9 in 985,747?

I have **3 hundred thousands
or 300,000.**

Who has the value of
400,000 + 7,000 + 600 + 2?

I have **9 hundred thousands
or 900,000.**

Who has the value of
40,000 + 7,000 + 600 + 2?

I have **407,602.**

Who has the value of the
5 in 75,923?

I Have, Who Has?: Math • 3–4 © 2006 Creative Teaching Press

Place Value 2

I have **5 thousands or 5,000.**

Who has the value of
90,000 + 2,000 + 300 + 60?

I have **75,200.**

Who has the value of the
2 in 240,760?

I have **92,360.**

Who has the value of the
5 in 567,812?

I have **2 hundred thousands
or 200,000.**

Who has the value of
3,000 + 500 + 9?

I have **5 hundred thousands
or 500,000.**

Who has the value of
700,000 + 50,000 + 200?

I have **3,509.**

Who has the value of the
7 in 973,114?

I have **750,200.**

Who has the value of the
3 in 738,459?

I have **7 ten thousands
or 70,000.**

Who has the value of
300,000 + 50,000 + 4,000?

I have **3 ten thousands
or 30,000.**

Who has the value of
70,000 + 5,000 + 200?

I have **354,000.**

Who has the value of the
9 in 394,552?

I Have, Who Has?: Math • 3–4 © 2006 Creative Teaching Press

Place Value 2

I have **9 ten thousands or 90,000.**

Who has the value of
10,000 + 900 + 80 + 2?

I have **83,027.**

Who has the value of the
8 in 981,200?

I have **10,982.**

Who has the value of the
6 in 670,912?

I have **8 ten thousands or 80,000.**

Who has the value of
800,000 + 30,000 + 2,000 + 7?

I have **6 hundred thousands or 600,000.**

Who has the value of
100,000 + 90,000 + 8,000 + 2?

I have **832,007.**

Who has the value of the
4 in 459,201?

I have **198,002.**

Who has the value of the
7 in 783,991?

I have **4 hundred thousands or 400,000.**

Who has the value of
400,000 + 9,000 + 300 + 20 + 9?

I have **7 hundred thousands or 700,000.**

Who has the value of
80,000 + 3,000 + 20 + 7?

I have **409,329.**

Who has the value of the
5 in 453,668?

Place Value 2

I have **5 ten thousands or 50,000.**

Who has the value of 80,000 + 300 + 40 + 6?

I have **654,200.**

Who has the value of 500,000 + 50,000 + 5,000 + 500 + 50 + 5?

I have **80,346.**

Who has the value of 800,000 + 30,000 + 4,000 + 600?

I have **555,555.**

Who has the value of the 1 in 713,900?

I have **834,600.**

Who has the value of the 1 in 139,880?

I have **1 ten thousand or 10,000.**

Who has the value of 200,000 + 50,000 + 400 + 2?

I have **1 hundred thousand or 100,000.**

Who has the value of 60,000 + 500 + 40 + 2?

I have **250,402.**

Who has the value of 70,000 + 4,000 + 300 + 60 + 5?

I have **60,542.**

Who has the value of 600,000 + 50,000 + 4,000 + 200?

I have **74,365.**

Who has the first card?

I Have, Who Has?: Math • 3–4 © 2006 Creative Teaching Press

Place Value 2

Directions: Complete the maze by highlighting the answers as your classmates identify them.

1 hundred thousand or 100,000	834,600	80,346	56,889	2 ten thousands or 20,000	8 hundred thousands or 800,000	4 ten thousands or 40,000
60,542	409,329	5 ten thousands or 50,000	47,602	9 hundred thousands or 900,000	582,110	**Start** *
654,200	4 hundred thousands or 400,000	925,360	6 ten thousands or 60,000	534,299	48,992	774,294
555,555	832,007	3 hundred thousands or 300,000	407,602	5 thousands or 5,000	92,360	201,101
1 ten thousand or 10,000	8 ten thousands or 80,000	83,027	7 hundred thousands or 700,000	198,002	5 hundred thousands or 500,000	750,200
250,402	24,550	981,203	39,702	6 hundred thousands or 600,000	846,294	3 ten thousands or 30,000
Finish 74,365	444,301	402,309	9 ten thousands or 90,000	10,982	384,927	75,200
430,998	20,909	723,948	354,000	7 ten thousands or 70,000	3,509	2 hundred thousands or 200,000

Choose four boxes that are **not** highlighted. Write each number in expanded form.

1. _____

2. _____

3. _____

4. _____

Making Sets of Ten

I have the **first card.**

Who has the answer to
25 + 10 − 3 − 20?

I have **24.**

Who has the answer to
55 + 15 + 12 − 32?

I have **12.**

Who has the answer to
100 − 25 + 3 − 8 + 20?

I have **50.**

Who has the answer to
91 − 11 − 20 − 15 + 2?

I have **90.**

Who has the answer to
38 + 12 − 30 + 7?

I have **47.**

Who has the answer to
51 + 19 + 3 − 13?

I have **27.**

Who has the answer to
71 + 19 − 40 + 1?

I have **60.**

Who has the answer to
43 − 13 − 15 + 4?

I have **51.**

Who has the answer to
22 + 18 + 4 − 20?

I have **19.**

Who has the answer to
21 + 19 + 4 + 20?

I Have, Who Has?: Math • 3–4 © 2006 Creative Teaching Press

Making Sets of Ten

I have **64.**

Who has the answer to
33 + 7 − 20 + 18?

I have **53.**

Who has the answer to
47 + 13 − 20 + 9?

I have **38.**

Who has the answer to
12 + 18 + 7 + 3?

I have **49.**

Who has the answer to
34 + 16 − 30 + 1?

I have **40.**

Who has the answer to
37 + 13 + 5 − 25?

I have **21.**

Who has the answer to
19 + 11 + 3 − 13?

I have **30.**

Who has the answer to
24 + 6 + 9 + 6?

I have **20.**

Who has the answer to
16 + 14 − 20 + 4?

I have **45.**

Who has the answer to
88 − 18 − 20 + 3?

I have **14.**

Who has the answer to
77 − 17 − 30 − 22?

Making Sets of Ten

I have **8.**

Who has the answer to
19 + 11 + 30 + 3?

I have **17.**

Who has the answer to
28 + 12 + 40 + 4?

I have **63.**

Who has the answer to
13 + 17 − 20 + 1?

I have **84.**

Who has the answer to
100 − 40 + 6 + 14?

I have **11.**

Who has the answer to
27 + 13 + 4 − 10?

I have **80.**

Who has the answer to
100 − 15 − 35 + 2?

I have **34.**

Who has the answer to
69 + 11 − 30 + 8?

I have **52.**

Who has the answer to
54 + 16 + 12 + 5?

I have **58.**

Who has the answer to
22 + 18 − 30 + 7?

I have **87.**

Who has the answer to
65 + 15 + 12 + 3?

I Have, Who Has?: Math • 3–4 © 2006 Creative Teaching Press

Making Sets of Ten

I have **95.**

Who has the answer to
55 + 15 + 16 + 14?

I have **67.**

Who has the answer to
28 + 12 + 4 + 10?

I have **100.**

Who has the answer to
47 + 13 + 15 + 2?

I have **54.**

Who has the answer to
41 + 19 + 5 − 40?

I have **77.**

Who has the answer to
59 + 11 − 20 + 41?

I have **25.**

Who has the answer to
76 + 4 + 9 − 30?

I have **91.**

Who has the answer to
77 + 13 + 9 − 20?

I have **59.**

Who has the answer to
8 + 12 + 22 + 20?

I have **79.**

Who has the answer to
39 + 11 + 7 + 10?

I have **62.**

Who has the first card?

Making Sets of Ten

Directions: As your classmates identify the answers, highlight each number in the grid below.

Why do potatoes make good detectives?

1 R	2 B	3 T	4 E	5 H	6 C	7 Y	8 C	9 A	10 A
11 N	12 O	13 T	14 S	15 I	16 U	17 S	18 S	19 K	20 L
21 O	22 E	23 M	24 C	25 R	26 T	27 U	28 H	29 P	30 E
31 S	32 E	33 T	34 R	35 M	36 Y	37 A	38 W	39 B	40 J
41 O	42 K	43 A	44 E	45 N	46 E	47 S	48 P	49 O	50 M
51 S	52 P	53 H	54 A	55 I	56 T	57 L	58 C	59 O	60 H
61 H	62 E	63 I	64 U	65 S	66 H	67 A	68 E	69 L	70 I
71 O	72 R	73 V	74 E	75 E	76 Y	77 R	78 E	79 Y	80 S
81 O	82 S	83 U	84 L	85 N	86 P	87 T	88 E	89 V	90 M
91 I	92 E	93 L	94 L	95 L	96 E	97 E	98 D	99 A	100 I

Follow these directions to reveal the answer to the riddle.

1. Cross out all the odd numbers that you did **not** highlight.
2. Write the letters in the boxes that are **not** highlighted or crossed out on the blanks below. Write the letters from left to right and top to bottom.

___ ___ ___ ___ ___ ___ ___   ___ ___ ___ ___ ___ ___

___ ___ ___ ___ ___ ___ ___   ___ ___ ___ ___

I Have, Who Has?: Math • 3–4 © 2006 Creative Teaching Press

Multiplication 1

I have the **first card.**

Who has the product of 2 × 5?

I have **60.**

Who has the product of 5 × 4?

I have **10.**

Who has the product of 5 × 8?

I have **20.**

Who has the product of 1 × 7?

I have **40.**

Who has the product of 2 × 2?

I have **7.**

Who has the product of 2 × 3?

I have **4.**

Who has the product of 5 × 5?

I have **6.**

Who has the product of 5 × 7?

I have **25.**

Who has the product of 10 × 6?

I have **35.**

Who has the product of 1 × 3?

Multiplication 1

I have **3.**

Who has the product of 5 × 6?

I have **15.**

Who has the product of 2 × 7?

I have **30.**

Who has the product of 2 × 4?

I have **14.**

Who has the product of 5 × 9?

I have **8.**

Who has the product of 10 × 9?

I have **45.**

Who has the product of 2 × 1?

I have **90.**

Who has the product of 2 × 6?

I have **2.**

Who has the product of 5 × 10?

I have **12.**

Who has the product of 5 × 3?

I have **50.**

Who has the product of 4 × 4?

I Have, Who Has?: Math • 3–4 © 2006 Creative Teaching Press

Multiplication 1

I have **16**.

Who has the product of 1 × 9?

I have **70**.

Who has the product of 4 × 6?

I have **9**.

Who has the product of 1 × 5?

I have **24**.

Who has the product of 2 × 9?

I have **5**.

Who has the product of 10 × 0?

I have **18**.

Who has the product of 10 × 8?

I have **0**.

Who has the product of 4 × 9?

I have **80**.

Who has the product of 4 × 7?

I have **36**.

Who has the product of 10 × 7?

I have **28**.

Who has the product of 4 × 8?

Multiplication 1

I have **32.**

Who has the product of 1×1?

I have **31.**

Who has the answer to $5 \times 5 + 1$?

I have **1.**

Who has the product of 10×10?

I have **26.**

Who has the answer to $10 \times 10 - 1$?

I have **100.**

Who has the product of 1×11?

I have **99.**

Who has the answer to $5 \times 10 + 1$?

I have **11.**

Who has the answer to $2 \times 10 + 1$?

I have **51.**

Who has the answer to $5 \times 10 - 1$?

I have **21.**

Who has the answer to $3 \times 10 + 1$?

I have **49.**

Who has the first card?

I Have, Who Has?: Math • 3–4 © 2006 Creative Teaching Press

Multiplication 1

Directions: As your classmates identify the answers, write each number in the grid from left to right and top to bottom.

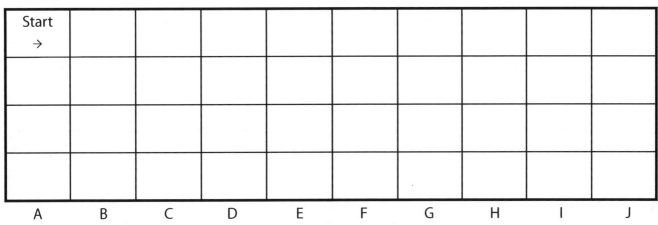

Start →									
A	B	C	D	E	F	G	H	I	J

Write each number in columns C, E, and J after the equals signs below. Create a multiplication fact for each number. The first one is done for you.

Column C

$\underline{\quad 5 \quad} \times \underline{\quad 8 \quad} = \underline{\quad 40 \quad}$

$\underline{\qquad} \times \underline{\qquad} = \underline{\quad 8 \quad}$

$\underline{\qquad} \times \underline{\qquad} = \underline{\qquad}$

$\underline{\qquad} \times \underline{\qquad} = \underline{\qquad}$

Column E

$\underline{\qquad} \times \underline{\qquad} = \underline{\qquad}$

$\underline{\qquad} \times \underline{\qquad} = \underline{\qquad}$

$\underline{\qquad} \times \underline{\qquad} = \underline{\qquad}$

$\underline{\qquad} \times \underline{\qquad} = \underline{\qquad}$

Column J

$\underline{\qquad} \times \underline{\qquad} = \underline{\qquad}$

$\underline{\qquad} \times \underline{\qquad} = \underline{\qquad}$

$\underline{\qquad} \times \underline{\qquad} = \underline{\qquad}$

$\underline{\qquad} \times \underline{\qquad} = \underline{\qquad}$

What is the sum of all the numbers in Column E? _____

Write an equation that equals that sum in the space below.

Multiplication 2

I have the **first card.**

Who has the product of 5 × 5?

I have **9.**

Who has the product of 4 × 2?

I have **25.**

Who has the product of 3 × 4?

I have **8.**

Who has the product of 3 × 2?

I have **12.**

Who has the product of 6 × 3?

I have **6.**

Who has the product of 5 × 3?

I have **18.**

Who has the product of 10 × 3?

I have **15.**

Who has the product of 10 × 7?

I have **30.**

Who has the product of 3 × 3?

I have **70.**

Who has the product of 5 × 4?

I Have, Who Has?: Math • 3–4 © 2006 Creative Teaching Press

Multiplication 2

I have **20.**

Who has the product of 3 × 8?

I have **35.**

Who has the product of 6 × 7?

I have **24.**

Who has the product of 6 × 6?

I have **42.**

Who has the product of 5 × 1?

I have **36.**

Who has the product of 10 × 1?

I have **5.**

Who has the product of 3 × 7?

I have **10.**

Who has the product of 4 × 4?

I have **21.**

Who has the product of 4 × 8?

I have **16.**

Who has the product of 5 × 7?

I have **32.**

Who has the product of 4 × 1?

Multiplication 2

I have **4.**

Who has the product of 5 × 8?

I have **48.**

Who has the product of 4 × 7?

I have **40.**

Who has the product of 5 × 10?

I have **28.**

Who has the product of 5 × 9?

I have **50.**

Who has the product of 3 × 1?

I have **45.**

Who has the product of 6 × 10?

I have **3.**

Who has the product of 3 × 9?

I have **60.**

Who has the product of 6 × 9?

I have **27.**

Who has the product of 6 × 8?

I have **54.**

Who has the product of 10 × 8?

I Have, Who Has?: Math • 3–4 © 2006 Creative Teaching Press

I have **80.**

Who has the product of 9 × 10?

I have **26.**

Who has the answer to 3 × 7 + 1?

I have **90.**

Who has the product of 10 × 10?

I have **22.**

Who has the answer to 6 × 6 + 1?

I have **100.**

Who has the answer to 3 × 4 + 1?

I have **37.**

Who has the answer to 6 × 5 + 1?

I have **13.**

Who has the answer to 3 × 6 + 1?

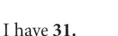

I have **31.**

Who has the answer to 6 × 7 – 1?

I have **19.**

Who has the answer to 3 × 9 – 1?

I have **41.**

Who has the first card?

Multiplication 2

Directions: As your classmates identify the answers, write each number in the grid from left to right and top to bottom.

Start →									

A　　B　　C　　D　　E　　F　　G　　H　　I　　J

Write each number in columns B, C, and G after the equals signs below. Create a multiplication fact for each number. The first one is done for you.

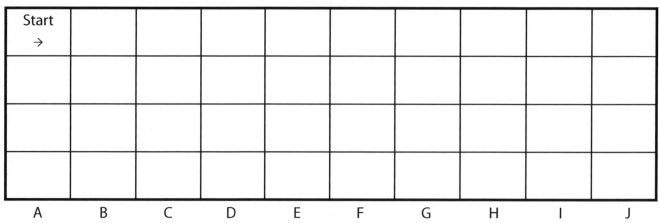

Column B

_____5___ × _____5___ = ___25___

_____ × _____ = ___24___

_____ × _____ = _____

_____ × _____ = _____

Column C

_____ × _____ = _____

_____ × _____ = _____

_____ × _____ = _____

_____ × _____ = _____

Column G

_____ × _____ = _____

_____ × _____ = _____

_____ × _____ = _____

_____ × _____ = _____

What is the sum of all the numbers in Column G? _____

Write an equation that equals that sum in the space below.

I Have, Who Has?: Math • 3–4 © 2006 Creative Teaching Press

Multiplication 3

I have the **first card.**

Who has the product of 7 × 6?

I have **30.**

Who has the product of 3 × 3?

I have **42.**

Who has the product of 8 × 8?

I have **9.**

Who has the product of 7 × 3?

I have **64.**

Who has the product of 6 × 3?

I have **21.**

Who has the product of 8 × 2?

I have **18.**

Who has the product of 4 × 3?

I have **16.**

Who has the product of 7 × 5?

I have **12.**

Who has the product of 6 × 5?

I have **35.**

Who has the product of 3 × 5?

Multiplication 3

I have **15.**

Who has the product of 4 × 5?

I have **63.**

Who has the product of 3 × 9?

I have **20.**

Who has the product of 8 × 3?

I have **27.**

Who has the product of 7 × 4?

I have **24.**

Who has the product of 4 × 2?

I have **28.**

Who has the product of 8 × 5?

I have **8.**

Who has the product of 8 × 4?

I have **40.**

Who has the product of 7 × 10?

I have **32.**

Who has the product of 7 × 9?

I have **70.**

Who has the product of 3 × 2?

I Have, Who Has?: Math • 3–4 © 2006 Creative Teaching Press

Multiplication 3

I have **6.**

Who has the product of 5 × 5?

I have **54.**

Who has the product of 5 × 9?

I have **25.**

Who has the product of 6 × 6?

I have **45.**

Who has the product of 8 × 10?

I have **36.**

Who has the product of 7 × 2?

I have **80.**

Who has the product of 7 × 7?

I have **14.**

Who has the product of 8 × 6?

I have **49.**

Who has the product of 5 × 2?

I have **48.**

Who has the product of 6 × 9?

I have **10.**

Who has the product of 8 × 7?

Multiplication 3

I have **56.**

Who has the product of 8 × 9?

I have **4.**

Who has the answer to 7 × 7 + 10?

I have **72.**

Who has the product of 5 × 10?

I have **59.**

Who has the answer to 8 × 5 + 1?

I have **50.**

Who has the product of 7 × 1?

I have **41.**

Who has the answer to 8 × 4 + 1?

I have **7.**

Who has the product of 6 × 10?

I have **33.**

Who has the answer to 8 × 8 + 1?

I have **60.**

Who has the product of 4 × 1?

I have **65.**

Who has the first card?

I Have, Who Has?: Math • 3–4 © 2006 Creative Teaching Press

Multiplication 3

Directions: Complete the maze by highlighting the answers as your classmates identify them.

64	18	12	55	40	70	6	7	60	4	59
42	36	30	20	28	8	25	50	40	81	41
Start *	12	9	33	27	14	36	72	56	42	33
35	16	21	32	63	48	54	21	10	50	**Finish** 65
15	20	24	8	16	35	45	80	49	64	36

Cross out all the odd numbers that you did **not** highlight. Write each remaining number after an equals sign below. Create a multiplication equation for each number. The first one is done for you.

1. _____ × ___4___ = ___36___

2. _____ × _____ = _____

3. _____ × _____ = _____

4. _____ × _____ = _____

5. _____ × _____ = _____

6. _____ × _____ = _____

7. _____ × _____ = _____

8. _____ × _____ = _____

9. _____ × _____ = _____

10. _____ × _____ = _____

Multiplication 4

I have the **first card.**

Who has the product of 9 × 2?

I have **27.**

Who has the product of 8 × 4?

I have **18.**

Who has the product of 9 × 4?

I have **32.**

Who has the product of 7 × 5?

I have **36.**

Who has the product of 4 × 3?

I have **35.**

Who has the product of 3 × 7?

I have **12.**

Who has the product of 8 × 8?

I have **21.**

Who has the product of 8 × 9?

I have **64.**

Who has the product of 9 × 3?

I have **72.**

Who has the product of 2 × 10?

I Have, Who Has?: Math • 3–4 © 2006 Creative Teaching Press

Multiplication 4

I have **20.**

Who has the product of 3 × 5?

I have **9.**

Who has the product of 9 × 9?

I have **15.**

Who has the product of 9 × 7?

I have **81.**

Who has the product of 7 × 6?

I have **63.**

Who has the product of 8 × 3?

I have **42.**

Who has the product of 3 × 2?

I have **24.**

Who has the product of 4 × 4?

I have **6.**

Who has the product of 5 × 2?

I have **16.**

Who has the product of 3 × 3?

I have **10.**

Who has the product of 9 × 5?

I Have, Who Has?: Math • 3–4 © 2006 Creative Teaching Press

Multiplication 4

I have **45.**

Who has the product of 8 × 5?

I have **25.**

Who has the product of 6 × 5?

I have **40.**

Who has the product of 4 × 2?

I have **30.**

Who has the product of 8 × 7?

I have **8.**

Who has the product of 9 × 6?

I have **56.**

Who has the product of 8 × 6?

I have **54.**

Who has the product of 7 × 4?

I have **48.**

Who has the product of 7 × 10?

I have **28.**

Who has the product of 5 × 5?

I have **70.**

Who has the product of 4 × 1?

I Have, Who Has?: Math • 3–4 © 2006 Creative Teaching Press

Multiplication 4

I have **4.**

Who has the product of 7 × 7?

I have **14.**

Who has the product of 8 × 10?

I have **49.**

Who has the product of 9 × 10?

I have **80.**

Who has the answer to 9 × 9 + 1?

I have **90.**

Who has the product of 5 × 1?

I have **82.**

Who has the answer to 9 × 8 + 1?

I have **5.**

Who has the product of 3 × 1?

I have **73.**

Who has the answer to 9 × 6 + 1?

I have **3.**

Who has the product of 7 × 2?

I have **55.**

Who has the first card?

I Have, Who Has? Math • 3–4 © 2006 Creative Teaching Press

Multiplication 4

Directions: As your classmates identify the answers, highlight each number in the grid below.

What did the beach say when the tide came in?

1 L	2 M	3 T	4 O	5 H	6 C	7 O	8 C	9 A	10 M
11 E	12 O	13 N	14 S	15 I	16 U	17 G	18 S	19 K	20 A
21 U	22 E	23 T	24 C	25 R	26 T	27 U	28 H	29 P	30 W
31 P	32 E	33 T	34 R	35 M	36 Y	37 I	38 W	39 B	40 H
41 R	42 K	43 M	44 E	45 S	46 E	47 E	48 P	49 O	50 O
51 B	52 P	53 N	54 A	55 E	56 T	57 O	58 C	59 O	60 L
61 L	62 E	63 I	64 U	65 E	66 H	67 S	68 E	69 L	70 I
71 M	72 R	73 V	74 E	75 R	76 Y	77 R	78 E	79 Y	80 H
81 S	82 S	83 E	84 L	85 L	86 P	87 A	88 E	89 V	90 S

Follow these directions to reveal the answer to the riddle.

1. Cross out all the even numbers that you did not highlight.
2. Cross out all the numbers that are multiples of 5.
3. Cross out all the numbers that are multiples of 11.
4. Cross out all the numbers that have 1 in the ones place except the number 1.
5. Cross out all the numbers that have 9 in the ones place.
6. Write the letters in the boxes that are not highlighted or crossed out on the blanks below. Write the letters in order from left to right and top to bottom.

" _____ _____ _____ _____ !"

I Have, Who Has?: Math • 3–4 © 2006 Creative Teaching Press

Working with Doubles

I have the **first card.**

Who has the product of 6 × 6?

I have **49.**

Who has the product of 10 × 10?

I have **36.**

Who has the product of 9 × 9?

I have **100.**

Who has the product of 2 × 2?

I have **81.**

Who has the product of 4 × 4?

I have **4.**

Who has the product of 8 × 8?

I have **16.**

Who has the product of 5 × 5?

I have **64.**

Who has the product of 3 × 3?

I have **25.**

Who has the product of 7 × 7?

I have **9.**

Who has the product of 1 × 1?

Working with Doubles

I have **1.**

Who has the answer to $4 \times 4 - 1$?

I have **5.**

Who has the answer to $9 \times 9 - 10$?

I have **15.**

Who has the answer to $8 \times 8 + 1$?

I have **71.**

Who has the answer to $10 \times 10 - 10$?

I have **65.**

Who has the answer to $7 \times 7 - 10$?

I have **90.**

Who has the answer to $6 \times 6 + 1$?

I have **39.**

Who has the answer to $3 \times 3 + 10$?

I have **37.**

Who has the answer to $4 \times 4 - 10$?

I have **19.**

Who has the answer to $2 \times 2 + 1$?

I have **6.**

Who has the answer to $8 \times 8 + 10$?

I Have, Who Has?: Math • 3–4 © 2006 Creative Teaching Press

Working with Doubles

I have **74.**

Who has the answer to $3 \times 3 + 1$?

I have **14.**

Who has the answer to $1 \times 1 + 10$?

I have **10.**

Who has the answer to $7 \times 7 - 1$?

I have **11.**

Who has the answer to $10 \times 10 - 1$?

I have **48.**

Who has the answer to $9 \times 9 + 1$?

I have **99.**

Who has the answer to $6 \times 6 + 10$?

I have **82.**

Who has the answer to $5 \times 5 - 1$?

I have **46.**

Who has the answer to $4 \times 4 + 1$?

I have **24.**

Who has the answer to $2 \times 2 + 10$?

I have **17.**

Who has the answer to $2 \times 2 - 1$?

I have **3.**

Who has the answer to $9 \times 9 + 10$?

I have **2.**

Who has the answer to $9 \times 9 - 1$?

I have **91.**

Who has the answer to $10 \times 10 + 10$?

I have **80.**

Who has the answer to $7 \times 7 + 10$?

I have **110.**

Who has the answer to $8 \times 8 - 1$?

I have **59.**

Who has the answer to $8 \times 8 - 10$?

I have **63.**

Who has the answer to $10 \times 10 + 1$?

I have **54.**

Who has the answer to $7 \times 7 + 1$?

I have **101.**

Who has the answer to $1 \times 1 + 1$?

I have **50.**

Who has the first card?

I Have, Who Has?: Math • 3–4 © 2006 Creative Teaching Press

Working with Doubles

Directions: As your classmates identify the answers, write each number in the grid from left to right and top to bottom.

Red →									
Blue									
Pink									
Green									100

Write the doubles for each number in the red row. The first one is done for you.

_____6_____ × _____6_____ = _____36_____   _____ × _____ = _____

_____ × _____ = _____   _____ × _____ = _____

_____ × _____ = _____   _____ × _____ = _____

_____ × _____ = _____   _____ × _____ = _____

_____ × _____ = _____   _____ × _____ = _____

I have the **first card.**

Who has the answer to
$7 \times 4 + 10 - 3$?

I have **48.**

Who has the answer to
$5 \times 8 + 25 + 4$?

I have **35.**

Who has the answer to
$3 \times 10 + 7 - 4$?

I have **69.**

Who has the answer to
$7 \times 7 + 11 - 10$?

I have **33.**

Who has the answer to
$6 \times 6 + 20 - 1$?

I have **50.**

Who has the answer to
$6 \times 5 - 15 + 4$?

I have **55.**

Who has the answer to
$5 \times 9 + 25 + 7$?

I have **19.**

Who has the answer to
$2 \times 4 + 40 - 10$?

I have **77.**

Who has the answer to
$2 \times 9 - 10 + 40$?

I have **38.**

Who has the answer to
$3 \times 7 + 9 - 20$?

I Have, Who Has?: Math • 3–4 © 2006 Creative Teaching Press

I have **10.**

Who has the answer to
$4 \times 3 + 8 + 7$?

I have **42.**

Who has the answer to
$7 \times 5 + 15 - 20$?

I have **27.**

Who has the answer to
$5 \times 5 + 20 - 40$?

I have **30.**

Who has the answer to
$4 \times 7 + 12 + 5$?

I have **5.**

Who has the answer to
$4 \times 6 - 4 + 20$?

I have **45.**

Who has the answer to
$3 \times 3 + 11 + 4$?

I have **40.**

Who has the answer to
$3 \times 6 + 20 - 4$?

I have **24.**

Who has the answer to
$5 \times 2 + 50 + 3$?

I have **34.**

Who has the answer to
$5 \times 6 + 14 - 2$?

I have **63.**

Who has the answer to
$5 \times 9 - 20 - 5$?

I have **20.**

Who has the answer to
3 × 10 + 12 − 1?

I have **28.**

Who has the answer to
7 × 7 − 30 − 4?

I have **41.**

Who has the answer to
6 × 6 + 1 + 20?

I have **15.**

Who has the answer to
4 × 4 + 3 + 20?

I have **57.**

Who has the answer to
7 × 7 + 20 − 4?

I have **39.**

Who has the answer to
8 × 8 + 2 − 20?

I have **65.**

Who has the answer to
5 × 5 + 4 + 20?

I have **46.**

Who has the answer to
9 × 9 − 30 + 1?

I have **49.**

Who has the answer to
4 × 4 + 2 + 10?

I have **52.**

Who has the answer to
5 × 8 + 6 − 20?

I have **26.**

Who has the answer to
$6 \times 4 + 4 - 10$?

I have **83.**

Who has the answer to
$9 \times 10 + 9 - 10$?

I have **18.**

Who has the answer to
$7 \times 7 + 2 - 20$?

I have **89.**

Who has the answer to
$10 \times 10 - 15 + 1$?

I have **31.**

Who has the answer to
$4 \times 8 + 30 + 2$?

I have **86.**

Who has the answer to
$7 \times 10 + 9 + 20$?

I have **64.**

Who has the answer to
$3 \times 9 - 10 + 30$?

I have **99.**

Who has the answer to
$8 \times 8 + 30 + 6$?

I have **47.**

Who has the answer to
$5 \times 8 + 3 + 40$?

I have **100.**

Who has the first card?

Addition, Subtraction, and Multiplication

Directions: Complete the maze by highlighting the answers as your classmates identify them.

50	19	38	10	27	44	83	89	86	99	**Finish** 100	28
69	36	90	40	5	21	47	64	90	82	12	36
48	54	72	34	42	53	70	31	52	46	39	15
77	55	80	16	30	88	54	18	26	22	30	28
62	33	35	**Start** *	45	24	63	20	41	57	65	49

- Cross out all the multiples of 10 that you did **not** highlight in the maze.
- Cross out all the odd numbers that you did **not** highlight.
- Cross out all the multiples of 11.
- Write an addition, subtraction, or multiplication equation for each number you did **not** highlight or cross out. The first one is done for you.

1. 15 + 13 = 28 or 30 – 2 = 28 or 7 × 4 = 28

2. _____

3. _____

4. _____

5. _____

6. _____

7. _____

8. _____

9. _____

10. _____

I Have, Who Has?: Math • 3–4 © 2006 Creative Teaching Press

Division 1

I have the **first card.**

Who has the quotient of 100 ÷ 2?

I have **6.**

Who has the quotient of 88 ÷ 8?

I have **50.**

Who has the quotient of 81 ÷ 9?

I have **11.**

Who has the quotient of 32 ÷ 8?

I have **9.**

Who has the quotient of 144 ÷ 12?

I have **4.**

Who has the quotient of 30 ÷ 10?

I have **12.**

Who has the quotient of 60 ÷ 12?

I have **3.**

Who has the quotient of 21 ÷ 3?

I have **5.**

Who has the quotient of 48 ÷ 8?

I have **7.**

Who has the quotient of 30 ÷ 2?

Division 1

I have **15.**

Who has the quotient of 84 ÷ 2?

I have **23.**

Who has the quotient of 39 ÷ 3?

I have **42.**

Who has the quotient of 66 ÷ 3?

I have **13.**

Who has the quotient of 28 ÷ 2?

I have **22.**

Who has the quotient of 93 ÷ 3?

I have **14.**

Who has the quotient of 18 ÷ 9?

I have **31.**

Who has the quotient of 70 ÷ 2?

I have **2.**

Who has the quotient of 82 ÷ 2?

I have **35.**

Who has the quotient of 46 ÷ 2?

I have **41.**

Who has the quotient of 100 ÷ 10?

I Have, Who Has?: Math • 3–4 © 2006 Creative Teaching Press

Division 1

I have **10.**

Who has the quotient of 100 ÷ 4?

I have **16.**

Who has the quotient of 99 ÷ 3?

I have **25.**

Who has the quotient of 48 ÷ 2?

I have **33.**

Who has the quotient of 64 ÷ 2?

I have **24.**

Who has the quotient of 72 ÷ 9?

I have **32.**

Who has the quotient of 88 ÷ 2?

I have **8.**

Who has the quotient of 100 ÷ 5?

I have **44.**

Who has the quotient of 90 ÷ 2?

I have **20.**

Who has the quotient of 32 ÷ 2?

I have **45.**

Who has the quotient of 160 ÷ 4?

I have **40.**

Who has the quotient of 120 ÷ 4?

I have **26.**

Who has the quotient of 210 ÷ 3?

I have **30.**

Who has the quotient of 120 ÷ 2?

I have **70.**

Who has the quotient of 110 ÷ 2?

I have **60.**

Who has the quotient of 72 ÷ 2?

I have **55.**

Who has the quotient of 300 ÷ 4?

I have **36.**

Who has the quotient of 68 ÷ 2?

I have **75.**

Who has the quotient of 900 ÷ 9?

I have **34.**

Who has the quotient of 52 ÷ 2?

I have **100.**

Who has the first card?

I Have, Who Has?: Math • *3–4* © 2006 Creative Teaching Press

Division 1

Directions: As your classmates identify the answers, write each number in one of the nine empty bags below. Start with Bag 1. Go from left to right and top to bottom. After writing a number in Bag 9 begin again with Bag 1.

Bag 1  Bag 2  Bag 3

Bag 4 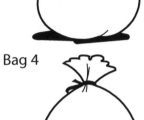 Bag 5  Bag 6

Bag 7 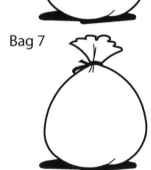 Bag 8  Bag 9

Use the numbers you recorded above to answer the questions below. Each bag holds the number of cans collected for a food drive.

1. What is the sum of all the numbers in Bag 4? _____

2. If all of the cans in Bag 4 are donated to three different shelters, how many cans will each shelter get? _____

3. What is the sum of all the numbers in Bag 7? _____

4. If the cans in Bag 7 are equally divided among eleven people, how many cans will be left over? _____

5. What is the sum of all the numbers in Bag 6? _____

6. If the cans in Bag 6 are equally divided among ten people, how many cans will each person receive? _____

I Have, Who Has? Math • 3–4 © 2006 Creative Teaching Press

Division 2

I have the **first card.**

Who has the quotient of 132 ÷ 12?

I have **10.**

Who has the quotient of 72 ÷ 9?

I have **11.**

Who has the quotient of 144 ÷ 12?

I have **8.**

Who has the quotient of 64 ÷ 4?

I have **12.**

Who has the quotient of 150 ÷ 75?

I have **16.**

Who has the quotient of 90 ÷ 6?

I have **2.**

Who has the quotient of 33 ÷ 11?

I have **15.**

Who has the quotient of 28 ÷ 2?

I have **3.**

Who has the quotient of 110 ÷ 11?

I have **14.**

Who has the quotient of 39 ÷ 3?

I Have, Who Has?: Math • 3–4 © 2006 Creative Teaching Press

Division 2

I have **13.**

Who has the quotient of 36 ÷ 9?

I have **51.**

Who has the quotient of 88 ÷ 4?

I have **4.**

Who has the quotient of 84 ÷ 12?

I have **22.**

Who has the quotient of 63 ÷ 3?

I have **7.**

Who has the quotient of 150 ÷ 6?

I have **21.**

Who has the quotient of 93 ÷ 3?

I have **25.**

Who has the quotient of 520 ÷ 10?

I have **31.**

Who has the quotient of 60 ÷ 12?

I have **52.**

Who has the quotient of 102 ÷ 2?

I have **5.**

Who has the quotient of 46 ÷ 2?

Division 2

I have **23.**

Who has the quotient of 99 ÷ 3?

I have **60.**

Who has the quotient of 300 ÷ 6?

I have **33.**

Who has the quotient of 64 ÷ 2?

I have **50.**

Who has the quotient of 120 ÷ 3?

I have **32.**

Who has the quotient of 200 ÷ 10?

I have **40.**

Who has the quotient of 52 ÷ 2?

I have **20.**

Who has the quotient of 320 ÷ 4?

I have **26.**

Who has the quotient of 48 ÷ 2?

I have **80.**

Who has the quotient of 180 ÷ 3?

I have **24.**

Who has the quotient of 68 ÷ 2?

I Have, Who Has?: Math • 3–4 © 2006 Creative Teaching Press

I have **34.**

Who has the quotient of 88 ÷ 2?

I have **35.**

Who has the quotient of 84 ÷ 2?

I have **44.**

Who has the quotient of 270 ÷ 9?

I have **42.**

Who has the quotient of 150 ÷ 2?

I have **30.**

Who has the quotient of 81 ÷ 9?

I have **75.**

Who has the quotient of 140 ÷ 2?

I have **9.**

Who has the quotient of 72 ÷ 12?

I have **70.**

Who has the quotient of 1000 ÷ 10?

I have **6.**

Who has the quotient of 70 ÷ 2?

I have **100.**

Who has the first card?

Division 2

Directions: As your classmates identify the answers, highlight each number in the grid.

What did one toilet say to the other toilet?

1 S	2 A	3 M	4 I	5 R	6 O	7 O	8 W	9 N	10 R
11 M	12 L	13 N	14 I	15 I	16 N	17 G	18 D	19 K	20 A
21 A	22 E	23 T	24 C	25 R	26 T	27 U	28 Y	29 P	30 N
31 R	32 E	33 T	34 R	35 M	36 O	37 I	38 U	39 B	40 H
41 O	42 K	43 M	44 E	45 S	46 L	47 E	48 O	49 O	50 O
51 O	52 P	53 N	54 O	55 E	56 K	57 O	58 A	59 O	60 L
61 P	62 L	63 I	64 I	65 E	66 H	67 S	68 T	69 L	70 I
71 B	72 T	73 V	74 L	75 R	76 E	77 R	78 F	79 Y	80 H
81 A	82 L	83 E	84 U	85 L	86 S	87 A	88 E	89 V	90 S
91 O	92 H	93 I	94 E	95 T	96 D	97 A	98 H	99 N	100 S

Follow these directions to reveal the answer to the riddle.

1. Cross out all the odd numbers that you did **not** highlight.
2. Cross out all the numbers that can be divided by 11.
3. Cross out all the numbers that can be divided by 10.
4. Cross out the largest and the smallest numbers that are still in the grid.
5. Write the letters in the boxes that are **not** highlighted or crossed out on the blanks below. Write the letters in order from left to right and top to bottom.

" ____ ____ ____ ____   ____ ____ ____ ____   ____   ____ ____ ____ ____ ____ ____

____ ____ ____ ____ ____ ____ ____ !"

I Have, Who Has?: Math • 3–4 © 2006 Creative Teaching Press

Basic Operations

I have the **first card.**

Who has the answer to
$100 \div 4 + 10 - 1$?

I have **6.**

Who has the answer to
$36 \div 4 \times 9 - 1$?

I have **34.**

Who has the answer to
$49 \div 7 + 10 - 1$?

I have **80.**

Who has the answer to
$10 \div 5 \times 9 + 20$?

I have **16.**

Who has the answer to
$80 \div 8 \times 5 + 3$?

I have **38.**

Who has the answer to
$18 \div 3 \times 5 \times 2$?

I have **53.**

Who has the answer to
$7 \times 7 + 20 - 1$?

I have **60.**

Who has the answer to
$7 \times 7 + 10 - 1$?

I have **68.**

Who has the answer to
$20 \div 5 \times 4 - 10$?

I have **58.**

Who has the answer to
$24 \div 3 \times 8 - 10$?

Basic Operations

I have **54.**

Who has the answer to
$9 \times 9 + 10$?

I have **24.**

Who has the answer to
$35 \div 5 \times 7$?

I have **91.**

Who has the answer to
$45 \div 5 \times 2 + 10$?

I have **49.**

Who has the answer to
$45 \div 5 \times 9$?

I have **28.**

Who has the answer to
$20 \div 5 \times 4 + 10$?

I have **81.**

Who has the answer to
$100 \div 10 \times 8 + 3$?

I have **26.**

Who has the answer to
$27 \div 3 \times 2 - 3$?

I have **83.**

Who has the answer to
$4 \times 9 \div 6 + 3$?

I have **15.**

Who has the answer to
$3 \times 2 \times 4$?

I have **9.**

Who has the answer to
$40 \div 8 \times 9$?

I Have, Who Has?: Math • 3–4 © 2006 Creative Teaching Press

Basic Operations

I have **45.**

Who has the answer to
$16 \div 2 \times 4$?

I have **40.**

Who has the answer to
$18 \div 2 \times 3$?

I have **32.**

Who has the answer to
$42 \div 7 \times 6 - 1$?

I have **27.**

Who has the answer to
$15 \div 3 \times 9 + 1$?

I have **35.**

Who has the answer to
$8 \times 8 + 20 - 2$?

I have **46.**

Who has the answer to
$48 \div 8 \times 6$?

I have **82.**

Who has the answer to
$70 \div 10 \times 3$?

I have **36.**

Who has the answer to
$2 \times 2 \times 8 + 20$?

I have **21.**

Who has the answer to
$56 \div 7 \times 5$?

I have **52.**

Who has the answer to
$7 \times 3 - 1 + 30$?

Basic Operations

I have **50.**

Who has the answer to
$8 \times 5 - 1 + 20$?

I have **4.**

Who has the answer to
$9 \div 3 \times 4$?

I have **59.**

Who has the answer to
$100 \div 4 \div 5$?

I have **12.**

Who has the answer to
$24 \div 8 \times 9 + 2$?

I have **5.**

Who has the answer to
$36 \div 6 \div 2$?

I have **29.**

Who has the answer to
$2 \times 5 \times 10$?

I have **3.**

Who has the answer to
$30 \div 6 \times 4$?

I have **100.**

Who has the answer to
$2 \times 2 \times 10 + 4$?

I have **20.**

Who has the answer to
$40 \div 5 \div 2$?

I have **44.**

Who has the first card?

I Have, Who Has?: Math • 3–4 © 2006 Creative Teaching Press

Basic Operations

Directions: As your classmates identify the answers, write each number in the grid from left to right and top to bottom.

Boat →										
Canoe										
Ship										
Yacht										1

Pick one of the water vehicles from the grid above. Write an equation with at least three steps for each number in that row. For example, if you choose "Boat," your first equation will equal 34; 20 – 5 + 19 = 34.

1. _____

2. _____

3. _____

4. _____

5. _____

6. _____

7. _____

8. _____

9. _____

10. _____

Balanced Equations 1

I have the **first card.**

Who has the equation that equals
144 ÷ 12?

I have **100 ÷ 10.**

Who has the equation that equals
12 × 4?

I have **3 × 4.**

Who has the equation that equals
9 × 8?

I have **6 × 8.**

Who has the equation that equals
180 ÷ 3?

I have **6 × 12.**

Who has the equation that equals
132 ÷ 12?

I have **15 × 4.**

Who has the equation that equals
2 × 50 − 4?

I have **88 ÷ 8.**

Who has the equation that equals
25 × 6?

I have **12 × 8.**

Who has the equation that equals
¼ of 100?

I have **75 × 2.**

Who has the equation that equals
110 ÷ 11?

I have **5 × 5.**

Who has the equation that equals
⅓ of 99?

I Have, Who Has?: Math • 3–4 © 2006 Creative Teaching Press

 # Balanced Equations 1

I have **3 × 11.**

Who has the equation that equals
½ of 88 ÷ 2?

I have **3 × 3 × 11.**

Who has the equation that equals
64 ÷ 8?

I have **11 × 2.**

Who has the equation that equals
3 × 12 – 1?

I have **2 × 2 × 2.**

Who has the equation that equals
42 ÷ 2 ÷ 3?

I have **5 × 7.**

Who has the equation that equals
¼ of 100 + 20?

I have **49 ÷ 7.**

Who has the equation that equals
32 ÷ 2?

I have **9 × 5.**

Who has the equation that equals
12 × 7?

I have **4 × 4.**

Who has the equation that equals
144 ÷ 12 ÷ 2?

I have **21 × 4.**

Who has the equation that equals
25 × 4 – 1?

I have **36 ÷ 6.**

Who has the equation that equals
3 × 12?

I Have, Who Has? Math • 3–4 © 2006 Creative Teaching Press

 # Balanced Equations 1

I have **6 × 6.**

Who has the equation that equals
5 × 8?

I have **84 ÷ 2.**

Who has the equation that equals
4 × 8?

I have **2 × 2 × 10.**

Who has the equation that equals
9 × 2?

I have **64 ÷ 2.**

Who has the equation that equals
12 × 2?

I have **3 × 6.**

Who has the equation that equals
60 ÷ 2 ÷ 6?

I have **6 × 4.**

Who has the equation that equals
90 ÷ 3?

I have **25 ÷ 5.**

Who has the equation that equals
7 × 9?

I have **6 × 5.**

Who has the equation that equals
100 ÷ 5?

I have **9 × 7.**

Who has the equation that equals
6 × 7?

I have **4 × 5.**

Who has the equation that equals
3 × 5?

I Have, Who Has?: Math • 3–4 © 2006 Creative Teaching Press

Balanced Equations 1

I have **30 ÷ 2.**

Who has the equation that equals
7 × 7?

I have **2 × 2 × 2 × 7.**

Who has the equation that equals
100 ÷ 2 + 5?

I have **100 ÷ 2 − 1.**

Who has the equation that equals
5 × 12 − 10?

I have **11 × 5.**

Who has the equation that equals
9 × 6?

I have **25 × 2.**

Who has the equation that equals
100 ÷ 5 + 1?

I have **3 × 3 × 3 × 2.**

Who has the equation that equals
3 × 9?

I have **3 × 7.**

Who has the equation that equals
9 × 9?

I have **5 × 5 + 2.**

Who has the equation that equals
4 × 7?

I have **8 × 11 − 7.**

Who has the equation that equals
7 × 8?

I have **6 × 5 − 2.**

Who has the first card?

Balanced Equations 1

Directions: As your classmates identify the numbers, highlight the correct equation. Choose the correct balanced equation for each row. When you are finished, choose ten equations that are **not** highlighted and write a new equation for each one. Write your equations on the back of the paper.

START 3×4	75×2
6×12	$49 \div 7$
4×5	$88 \div 8$
3×6	75×2
6×12	$100 \div 10$
6×8	$49 \div 7$
$84 \div 2$	15×4
12×8	3×4
5×5	$49 \div 7$
$5 \times 5 + 2$	3×11
11×2	25×2
4×5	5×7
$100 \div 10$	9×5
21×4	3×6
25×2	$3 \times 3 \times 11$
75×2	$2 \times 2 \times 2$
6×12	$49 \div 7$
4×4	$84 \div 2$
$36 \div 6$	6×12

6×6	$3 \times 3 \times 3 \times 2$
$8 \times 11 - 7$	$2 \times 2 \times 10$
3×6	75×2
$25 \div 5$	$100 \div 10$
$6 \times 5 - 1$	9×7
$100 \div 10$	$84 \div 2$
$64 \div 2$	5×5
3×4	6×4
6×12	6×5
$6 \times 5 - 1$	4×5
$2 \times 2 \times 2$	$30 \div 2$
$100 \div 2 - 1$	$36 \div 6$
$3 \times 3 \times 11$	25×2
3×7	$5 \times 5 + 2$
$8 \times 11 - 7$	5×5
$2 \times 2 \times 2 \times 7$	3×4
$49 \div 7$	11×5
$2 \times 2 \times 2$	$3 \times 3 \times 3 \times 2$
$5 \times 5 + 2$	$36 \div 6$
FINISH $100 \div 10$	$6 \times 5 - 2$

I Have, Who Has?: Math • 3–4 © 2006 Creative Teaching Press

 # Balanced Equations 2

I have the **first card.**

Who has the equation that equals
4 × 4 + 1?

I have **2 × 3.**

Who has the equation that equals
100 ÷ 25 ÷ 2?

I have **5 × 4 – 3.**

Who has the equation that equals
2 × 7?

I have **40 ÷ 20.**

Who has the equation that equals
132 ÷ 11?

I have **144 ÷ 12 + 2.**

Who has the equation that equals
16 ÷ 4?

I have **144 ÷ 12.**

Who has the equation that equals
7 × 3?

I have **32 ÷ 8.**

Who has the equation that equals
36 ÷ 12?

I have **4 × 5 + 1.**

Who has the equation that equals
5 × 6 + 1?

I have **75 ÷ 25.**

Who has the equation that equals
36 ÷ 6?

I have **7 × 5 – 4.**

Who has the equation that equals
3 × 5?

# Balanced Equations 2

I have **30 ÷ 2.**

Who has the equation that equals
$2 \times 6 + 1$?

I have **7 × 5 − 1.**

Who has the equation that equals
4×11?

I have **4 × 3 + 1.**

Who has the equation that equals
7×7?

I have **5 × 9 − 1.**

Who has the equation that equals
$6 \times 9 - 1$?

I have **5 × 10 − 1.**

Who has the equation that equals
$12 \times 5 - 1$?

I have **5 × 10 + 3.**

Who has the equation that equals
$100 \div 4 \times 3$?

I have **5 × 11 + 4.**

Who has the equation that equals
$100 \div 4$?

I have **7 × 11 − 2.**

Who has the equation that equals
8×8?

I have **5 × 5.**

Who has the equation that equals
$4 \times 8 + 2$?

I have **12 × 5 + 4.**

Who has the equation that equals
$2 \times 2 \times 2 \times 3$?

I Have, Who Has?: Math • 3–4 © 2006 Creative Teaching Press

I have **12 × 2.**

Who has the equation that equals
4 × 11 − 1?

I have **3 × 3.**

Who has the equation that equals
45 ÷ 9?

I have **6 × 7 + 1.**

Who has the equation that equals
3 × 3 × 2?

I have **100 ÷ 20.**

Who has the equation that equals
44 ÷ 2?

I have **6 × 3.**

Who has the equation that equals
64 ÷ 8?

I have **4 × 5 + 2.**

Who has the equation that equals
8 × 5 + 1?

I have **96 ÷ 12.**

Who has the equation that equals
49 ÷ 7?

I have **25 × 2 − 9.**

Who has the equation that equals
6 × 6 + 1?

I have **2 × 2 × 2 − 1.**

Who has the equation that equals
81 ÷ 9?

I have **8 × 5 − 3.**

Who has the equation that equals
2 × 2 × 5?

Balanced Equations 2

I have **100 ÷ 5.**

Who has the equation that equals
11 × 5?

I have **5 × 10 − 2.**

Who has the equation that equals
100 ÷ 10?

I have **6 × 9 + 1.**

Who has the equation that equals
3 × 3 × 7?

I have **3 × 3 + 1.**

Who has the equation that equals
121 ÷ 11?

I have **6 × 11 − 3.**

Who has the equation that equals
3 × 11?

I have **77 ÷ 7.**

Who has the equation that equals
2 × 12 − 1?

I have **8 × 4 + 1.**

Who has the equation that equals
6 × 4 + 2?

I have **6 × 4 − 1.**

Who has the equation that equals
2 × 2 × 8?

I have **50 ÷ 2 + 1.**

Who has the equation that equals
6 × 8?

I have **3 × 10 + 2.**

Who has the first card?

I Have, Who Has!: Math • 3–4 © 2006 Creative Teaching Press

Balanced Equations 2

Directions: Complete the maze by highlighting the answers as your classmates identify them.

A	B	C	D
2×3	$40 \div 20$	$6 \times 4 - 1$	$3 \times 10 + 2$ **Finish**
$5 \times 10 - 2$	$3 \times 3 + 1$	$77 \div 7$	$7 \times 5 - 4$
$50 \div 2 + 1$	$8 \times 4 + 1$	$6 \times 11 - 3$	$6 \times 9 + 1$
$144 \div 12$	$5 \times 11 + 4$	$3 \times 10 + 2$	$100 \div 5$
6×3	$96 \div 12$	$2 \times 2 \times 2 - 1$	$8 \times 5 - 3$
$6 \times 7 + 1$	12×2	3×3	$25 \times 2 - 9$
$75 \div 25$	$12 \times 5 + 4$	$100 \div 20$	$4 \times 5 + 2$
$32 \div 8$	$7 \times 11 - 2$	2×3	$5 \times 10 + 3$
$30 \div 2$	$5 \times 10 + 3$	$6 \times 9 + 1$	12×2
$7 \times 5 - 1$	$5 \times 9 - 1$	$3 \times 3 + 1$	$77 \div 7$
5×5	$4 \times 3 + 1$	$30 \div 2$	$3 \times 10 - 2$
$5 \times 11 + 4$	$5 \times 10 - 1$	$7 \times 5 - 4$	$4 \times 5 + 1$
$7 \times 5 - 4$	$3 \times 10 + 2$	6×3	$144 \div 12$
$5 \times 4 - 3$	$144 \div 12 + 2$	$32 \div 8$	$40 \div 20$
Start *	2×3	$75 \div 25$	2×3

Write equations that balance with each of the six equations **not** highlighted in Column A of the maze. The first one is done for you.

1. ____ 2×3 ____ = ____ $2 \times 2 + 2$ ____

2. _____ = _____

3. _____ = _____

4. _____ = _____

5. _____ = _____

6. _____ = _____

 # Comparing Fractions

I have the **first card.**

Who has the fraction that is smaller:
½ or ⅔ ?

I have ¹⁄₁₅.

Who has the fraction that is greater:
³⁄₂₀ or ³⁄₇?

I have ½.

Who has the fraction that is greater:
⁵⁄₉ or ²⁄₇?

I have ³⁄₇.

Who has the fraction that is smaller:
¹⁄₁₂ or ⅙?

I have ⁵⁄₉.

Who has the fraction that is smaller:
⅔ or ⅞?

I have ¹⁄₁₂.

Who has the fraction that is greater:
⅛ or ²⁄₅?

I have ⅔.

Who has the fraction that is greater:
³⁄₅ or ²⁄₇?

I have ²⁄₅.

Who has the fraction that is smaller:
³⁄₂₀ or ⁴⁄₇?

I have ³⁄₅.

Who has the fraction that is smaller:
³⁄₇ or ¹⁄₁₅?

I have ³⁄₂₀.

Who has the fraction that is greater:
¼ or ⅓?

I Have, Who Has?: Math • 3–4 © 2006 Creative Teaching Press

 # Comparing Fractions

I have ⅓.

Who has the fraction that is smaller:
⁵⁄₇ or ⁵⁄₁₂?

I have ³⁄₁₀.

Who has the fraction that is greater:
¹⁄₁₀ or ²⁄₇?

I have ⁵⁄₁₂.

Who has the fraction that is greater:
⁶⁄₇ or ⅜?

I have ²⁄₇.

Who has the fraction that is smaller:
⅚ or ²⁄₉?

I have ⁶⁄₇.

Who has the fraction that is smaller:
²⁄₁₅ or ²⁄₇?

I have ²⁄₉.

Who has the fraction that is greater:
¾ or ⁷⁄₁₂?

I have ²⁄₁₅.

Who has the fraction that is greater:
¹⁷⁄₂₀ or ⁹⁄₁₀?

I have ¾.

Who has the fraction that is smaller:
⅜ or ⁷⁄₁₂?

I have ⁹⁄₁₀.

Who has the fraction that is smaller:
³⁄₁₀ or ⅘?

I have ⅜.

Who has the fraction that is greater:
¼ or ⅕?

Comparing Fractions

I have ¼.

Who has the fraction that is smaller:
⅙ or ⅐?

I have ⅘.

Who has the fraction that is smaller:
⁷⁄₁₂ or ⅑?

I have ⅐.

Who has the fraction that is greater:
⅛ or ⅑?

I have ⅑.

Who has the fraction that is greater:
¹⁷⁄₂₀ or ⁴⁄₇?

I have ⅛.

Who has the fraction that is smaller:
⅕ or ⅙?

I have ¹⁷⁄₂₀.

Who has the fraction that is smaller:
¹⁄₁₀ or ⅕?

I have ⅙.

Who has the fraction that is greater:
⅝ or ⅚?

I have ¹⁄₁₀.

Who has the fraction that is greater:
⅝ or ¹¹⁄₁₂?

I have ⅚.

Who has the fraction that is greater:
⅘ or ⁴⁄₉?

I have ¹¹⁄₁₂.

Who has the fraction that is smaller:
⁸⁄₉ or ⁷⁄₁₂?

I Have, Who Has?: Math • 3–4 © 2006 Creative Teaching Press

 # Comparing Fractions

I have $\frac{7}{12}$.

Who has the fraction that is greater:
$\frac{7}{10}$ or $\frac{4}{7}$?

I have $\frac{7}{8}$.

Who has the fraction that is smaller:
$\frac{5}{7}$ or $\frac{4}{7}$?

I have $\frac{7}{10}$.

Who has the fraction that is smaller:
$\frac{4}{9}$ or $\frac{5}{7}$?

I have $\frac{4}{7}$.

Who has the fraction that is greater:
$\frac{5}{8}$ or $\frac{5}{7}$?

I have $\frac{4}{9}$.

Who has the fraction that is greater:
$\frac{8}{9}$ or $\frac{5}{8}$?

I have $\frac{5}{7}$.

Who has the fraction that is smaller:
$\frac{5}{8}$ or $\frac{1}{20}$?

I have $\frac{8}{9}$.

Who has the fraction that is smaller:
$\frac{1}{5}$ or $\frac{5}{7}$?

I have $\frac{1}{20}$.

Who has the fraction that is greater:
$\frac{7}{9}$ or $\frac{4}{9}$?

I have $\frac{1}{5}$.

Who has the fraction that is greater:
$\frac{7}{8}$ or $\frac{7}{9}$?

I have $\frac{7}{9}$.

Who has the first card?

Comparing Fractions

Directions: As your classmates identify the answers, highlight or cross out each fraction.

$\dfrac{3}{8}$	$\dfrac{5}{12}$	$\dfrac{1}{6}$	$\dfrac{3}{20}$	$\dfrac{4}{9}$	$\dfrac{3}{4}$	$\dfrac{3}{7}$	$\dfrac{17}{20}$	$\dfrac{2}{9}$
$\dfrac{7}{10}$	$\dfrac{1}{7}$	$\dfrac{1}{2}$	$\dfrac{5}{8}$	$\dfrac{2}{5}$	$\dfrac{1}{20}$	$\dfrac{9}{10}$	$\dfrac{3}{11}$	$\dfrac{5}{9}$
$\dfrac{1}{15}$	$\dfrac{4}{5}$	$\dfrac{6}{7}$	$\dfrac{3}{10}$	$\dfrac{7}{12}$	$\dfrac{1}{4}$	$\dfrac{2}{6}$	$\dfrac{1}{8}$	$\dfrac{4}{7}$
$\dfrac{9}{11}$	$\dfrac{2}{15}$	$\dfrac{4}{11}$	$\dfrac{5}{6}$	$\dfrac{2}{3}$	$\dfrac{1}{5}$	$\dfrac{1}{3}$	$\dfrac{1}{9}$	$\dfrac{7}{8}$
$\dfrac{5}{7}$	$\dfrac{1}{10}$	$\dfrac{1}{12}$	$\dfrac{7}{9}$	$\dfrac{8}{9}$	$\dfrac{2}{7}$	$\dfrac{7}{15}$	$\dfrac{3}{5}$	$\dfrac{11}{12}$

Write the six fractions you did **not** highlight in the middle column of the chart. Then write one fraction that is greater and one that is smaller than each of these fractions.

Smaller Fraction	Leftover Fraction	Greater Fraction
<	<	
<	<	
<	<	
<	<	
<	<	
<	<	

I have the **first card**.

Who has the word that names the top part of a fraction?

I have **⁴/₉**.

Who has the sum of ¹/₁₁ and ³/₁₁?

I have the **numerator**.

Who has the word that names the answer to an addition problem?

I have **⁴/₁₁**.

Who has the difference between ³/₈ and ²/₈?

I have the **sum**.

Who has the word that names the bottom part of a fraction?

I have **¹/₈**.

Who has the difference between ¹⁷/₂₅ and ⁶/₂₅?

I have the **denominator**.

Who has the word that names the answer to a subtraction problem?

I have **¹¹/₂₅**.

Who has the sum of ¹/₆ and ⁴/₆?

I have the **difference**.

Who has the sum of ¹/₉ and ³/₉?

I have **⁵/₆**.

Who has the sum of ¼ and ²/₄?

Addition and Subtraction—Fractions

I have ¾.

Who has the difference between ⁷⁄₁₀ and ⁴⁄₁₀?

I have ¹⁄₇.

Who has the difference between ³⁄₅ and ²⁄₅?

I have ³⁄₁₀.

Who has the difference between ⁷⁄₉ and ²⁄₉?

I have ¹⁄₅.

Who has the sum of ²⁄₇ and ³⁄₇?

I have ⁵⁄₉.

Who has the sum of ¹⁄₅ and ³⁄₅?

I have ⁵⁄₇.

Who has the sum of ³⁄₁₀ and ³⁄₁₀ and ¹⁄₁₀?

I have ⁴⁄₅.

Who has the sum of ⅓ and ⅓?

I have ⁷⁄₁₀.

Who has the difference between ⁴⁄₇ and ¹⁄₇?

I have ⅔.

Who has the difference between ⁶⁄₇ and ⁵⁄₇?

I have ³⁄₇.

Who has the difference between ⁴⁄₅ and ²⁄₅?

Addition and Subtraction—Fractions

I have ²⁄₅.

Who has the sum of
¹⁄₉ and ⁷⁄₉?

I have ²⁄₄ or ½.

Who has the sum of
¹⁄₇ and ¹⁄₇?

I have ⁸⁄₉.

Who has the sum of
³⁄₈ and ¹⁄₈ and ¹⁄₈?

I have ²⁄₇.

Who has the difference between
⁵⁄₆ and ⁴⁄₆?

I have ⁵⁄₈.

Who has the difference between
⁵⁄₉ and ⁴⁄₉?

I have ¹⁄₆.

Who has the difference between
¹¹⁄₁₅ and ⁴⁄₁₅?

I have ¹⁄₉.

Who has the difference between
¹⁰⁄₁₁ and ¹⁄₁₁?

I have ⁷⁄₁₅.

Who has the sum of
²⁄₅ and ¹⁄₅?

I have ⁹⁄₁₁.

Who has the sum of
¼ and ¼?

I have ³⁄₅.

Who has the sum of
³⁄₈ and ³⁄₈ and ¹⁄₈?

I Have, Who Has?: Math • 3–4 © 2006 Creative Teaching Press

I have ⅞.

Who has the difference between ¾ and ²/₄?

I have ²/₉.

Who has the difference between ⅞ and ⁴/₈?

I have ¼.

Who has the difference between one whole and ⅔?

I have ⅜.

Who has the sum of ⁶/₁₂ and ¹/₁₂?

I have ⅓.

Who has the sum of ²/₁₁ and ⁵/₁₁?

I have ⁷/₁₂.

Who has the sum of ⁷/₁₀ and ²/₁₀?

I have ⁷/₁₁.

Who has the sum of ³/₁₂ and ¹/₁₂ and ¹/₁₂?

I have ⁹/₁₀.

Who has the difference between ⁶/₇ and ²/₇?

I have ⁵/₁₂.

Who has the difference between ⁷/₉ and ⁵/₉?

I have ⁴/₇.

Who has the first card?

Addition and Subtraction—Fractions

Directions: As your classmates identify the answers, highlight the correct word or fraction. Choose the correct answer for each row. On the back of this paper, write a fraction addition problem for every fraction **not** highlighted that can be divided by 5.

START	
numerator	denominator
sum	difference
denominator	numerator
sum	difference
2/9	4/9
4/11	6/11
1/8	3/8
13/25	11/25
1/6	5/6
3/4	1/4
3/10	7/10
5/9	7/9
3/5	4/5
2/3	1/3
1/7	4/7
1/5	2/5
5/7	2/7
7/10	3/10
1/7	3/7
3/5	2/5

8/9	2/9
5/8	3/8
7/9	1/9
3/11	9/11
1/4	2/4 or 1/2
2/7	5/7
1/6	5/6
7/15	11/15
4/5	3/5
7/8	2/8
3/4	1/4
2/3	1/3
5/11	7/11
5/12	11/12
2/9	4/9
3/8	1/8
5/12	7/12
9/10	3/10
4/7	3/7
FINISH Good	Thinking!

I Have, Who Has?: Math • 3–4 © 2006 Creative Teaching Press

I have the **first card.**

Who has the sum of 1²⁄₆ + 2³⁄₆?

I have **2⁴⁄₅.**

Who has the sum of 2¼ + 2¼?

I have **3⁵⁄₆.**

Who has the sum of 4⁵⁄₈ + 2²⁄₈?

I have **4²⁄₄ or 4½.**

Who has the sum of 3⅓ + 2⅓?

I have **6⁷⁄₈.**

Who has the sum of 1⅓ + ⅓?

I have **5⅔.**

Who has the sum of ⅔ + ⅓?

I have **1²⁄₃.**

Who has the sum of 2⅕ + 3²⁄₅?

I have **³⁄₃ or 1.**

Who has the sum of 2¾ + ¼?

I have **5³⁄₅.**

Who has the sum of 1³⁄₅ + 1¹⁄₅?

I have **2⁴⁄₄ or 3.**

Who has the sum of 1³⁄₆ + ²⁄₆?

I Have, Who Has?: Math • 3–4 © 2006 Creative Teaching Press

I have **1⅚.**

Who has the sum of 3⅘ + ⅕?

I have 5³⁄₆ **or 5½.**

Who has the difference of 6⅔ − 2⅓?

I have **3⁵⁄₅ or 4.**

Who has the sum of 3⅓ + 1⅓?

I have **4⅓.**

Who has the difference of 5⅘ − 2⅗?

I have **4⅔.**

Who has the sum of 2⅕ + 3⅗?

I have **3⅕.**

Who has the difference of 4⅔ − 1⅓?

I have **5⅘.**

Who has the sum of 2¼ + 1¼?

I have **3⅓.**

Who has the difference of 7⅘ − 4⅖?

I have **3²⁄₄ or 3½.**

Who has the sum of 2⅙ + 3²⁄₆?

I have **3⅖.**

Who has the sum of 1³⁄₇ + 1²⁄₇?

I have **2⁵⁄₇**.

Who has the difference of 6⁴⁄₅ – 5²⁄₅?

I have **1¼ or 2**.

Who has the sum of 2³⁄₇ + 2⁴⁄₇?

I have **1²⁄₅**.

Who has the difference of 7²⁄₃ – 5⅓?

I have **4⁷⁄₇ or 5**.

Who has the difference of 6⁴⁄₅ – 2¹⁄₅?

I have **2⅓**.

Who has the sum of 1¹⁄₆ + 1²⁄₆?

I have **4³⁄₅**.

Who has the difference of 5²⁄₃ – 4⅓?

I have **2³⁄₆ or 2½**.

Who has the difference of 4⁵⁄₆ – 3²⁄₆?

I have **1⅓**.

Who has the difference of 7⁴⁄₅ – 1³⁄₅?

I have **1³⁄₆ or 1½**.

Who has the sum of 1¼ + ¾?

I have **6¹⁄₅**.

Who has the difference of 4⁵⁄₆ – 2⁴⁄₆?

I have **2⅙.**

Who has the sum of 1⅜ + 3²⁄₈?

I have **4¹⁄₇.**

Who has the difference of 5⁷⁄₁₀ − 4⁶⁄₁₀?

I have **4⅝.**

Who has the sum of 6¼ + ¼?

I have **1¹⁄₁₀.**

Who has the sum of 3⅕ + 3⅕?

I have **6²⁄₄ or 6½.**

Who has the sum of 1¼ + 1²⁄₄?

I have **6⅖.**

Who has the difference of 7⅘ − 2⅖?

I have **2¾.**

Who has the sum of 3¼ + 2²⁄₄?

I have **5⅖.**

Who has the difference of 7⅔ − 1⅓?

I have **5¾.**

Who has the difference of 6⁶⁄₇ − 2⁵⁄₇?

I have **6⅓.**

Who has the first card?

Addition and Subtraction—Mixed Numbers

Directions: Complete the maze by highlighting the answers as your classmates identify them.

$6\frac{2}{5}$	$1\frac{1}{10}$	$2\frac{3}{4}$	$6\frac{2}{4}$ or $6\frac{1}{2}$	$2\frac{1}{4}$	$1\frac{1}{3}$	$4\frac{3}{5}$	$4\frac{7}{7}$ or 5	$2\frac{1}{2}$	$6\frac{2}{3}$
$5\frac{2}{5}$	$4\frac{1}{7}$	$5\frac{3}{4}$	$4\frac{5}{8}$	$2\frac{1}{6}$	$6\frac{1}{5}$	$1\frac{3}{6}$ or $1\frac{1}{2}$	$1\frac{4}{4}$ or 2	$7\frac{4}{5}$	$4\frac{4}{5}$
Finish $6\frac{1}{3}$	$5\frac{3}{5}$	$2\frac{4}{5}$	$4\frac{2}{4}$ or $4\frac{1}{2}$	$3\frac{1}{3}$	$4\frac{1}{5}$	$2\frac{3}{6}$ or $2\frac{1}{2}$	$2\frac{1}{3}$	$1\frac{2}{5}$	$7\frac{1}{2}$
$3\frac{4}{6}$	$1\frac{2}{3}$	9	$5\frac{2}{3}$	5	$1\frac{2}{3}$	$7\frac{1}{6}$	8	$2\frac{5}{7}$	$3\frac{1}{5}$
$3\frac{5}{6}$	$6\frac{7}{8}$	$2\frac{4}{4}$ or 3	$3\frac{3}{3}$ or 1	$4\frac{3}{8}$	$3\frac{2}{4}$ or $3\frac{1}{2}$	$5\frac{3}{6}$ or $5\frac{1}{2}$	$4\frac{1}{3}$	$3\frac{2}{5}$	$8\frac{1}{3}$
Start *	$3\frac{2}{3}$	$1\frac{5}{6}$	$3\frac{5}{5}$ or 4	$4\frac{2}{3}$	$5\frac{4}{5}$	6	$3\frac{1}{5}$	$3\frac{1}{3}$	7

- Cross out all the fractions **greater** than 3⅓ that you did **not** already highlight in the game.
- In the space below, write an addition or a subtraction problem using mixed fractions for each of the five fractions that are **not** highlighted or crossed out.

1. _____

2. _____

3. _____

4. _____

5. _____

I Have, Who Has?: Math • 3–4 © 2006 Creative Teaching Press

 # Changing Mixed Numbers to Decimals

I have the **first card.**

Who has the decimal equal to 4⁵/₁₀?

I have **2.3.**

Who has the decimal equal to 1⁷/₁₀?

I have **4.5.**

Who has the decimal equal to 2³³/₁₀₀?

I have **1.7.**

Who has the decimal equal to 3⁵/₁₀?

I have **2.33.**

Who has the decimal equal to 6³/₁₀?

I have **3.5.**

Who has the decimal equal to 5¹/₁₀?

I have **6.3.**

Who has the decimal equal to 5²⁵/₁₀₀?

I have **5.1.**

Who has the decimal equal to 3⁴⁵/₁₀₀?

I have **5.25.**

Who has the decimal equal to 2³/₁₀?

I have **3.45.**

Who has the decimal equal to 6⁸⁹/₁₀₀?

I Have, Who Has? Math • 3–4 © 2006 Creative Teaching Press

 # Changing Mixed Numbers to Decimals

I have **6.89.**

Who has the decimal equal to $4\frac{55}{100}$?

I have **3.66.**

Who has the decimal equal to $5\frac{29}{100}$?

I have **4.55.**

Who has the decimal equal to $1\frac{17}{100}$?

I have **5.29.**

Who has the decimal equal to $4\frac{7}{10}$?

I have **1.17.**

Who has the decimal equal to $5\frac{3}{10}$?

I have **4.7.**

Who has the decimal equal to $3\frac{1}{10}$?

I have **5.3.**

Who has the decimal equal to $1\frac{6}{10}$?

I have **3.1.**

Who has the decimal equal to $6\frac{9}{10}$?

I have **1.6.**

Who has the decimal equal to $3\frac{66}{100}$?

I have **6.9.**

Who has the decimal equal to $2\frac{2}{10}$?

I Have, Who Has?: Math • 3–4 © 2006 Creative Teaching Press

Changing Mixed Numbers to Decimals

I have **2.2.**

Who has the decimal equal to $1\frac{47}{100}$?

I have **4.1.**

Who has the decimal equal to $2\frac{99}{100}$?

I have **1.47.**

Who has the decimal equal to $4\frac{15}{100}$?

I have **2.99.**

Who has the decimal equal to $5\frac{13}{100}$?

I have **4.15.**

Who has the decimal equal to $6\frac{37}{100}$?

I have **5.13.**

Who has the decimal equal to $6\frac{7}{10}$?

I have **6.37.**

Who has the decimal equal to $1\frac{3}{10}$?

I have **6.7.**

Who has the decimal equal to $2\frac{7}{10}$?

I have **1.3.**

Who has the decimal equal to $4\frac{1}{10}$?

I have **2.7.**

Who has the decimal equal to $5\frac{9}{10}$?

Changing Mixed Numbers to Decimals

I have **5.9.**

Who has the decimal equal to $3^{27}/_{100}$?

I have **4.99.**

Who has the decimal equal to $6^2/_{10}$?

I have **3.27.**

Who has the decimal equal to $6^{71}/_{100}$?

I have **6.2.**

Who has the decimal equal to $1^5/_{10}$?

I have **6.71.**

Who has the decimal equal to $3^9/_{10}$?

I have **1.5.**

Who has the decimal equal to $2^{53}/_{100}$?

I have **3.9.**

Who has the decimal equal to $1^{88}/_{100}$?

I have **2.53.**

Who has the decimal equal to $3^7/_{10}$?

I have **1.88.**

Who has the decimal equal to $4^{99}/_{100}$?

I have **3.7.**

Who has the first card?

I Have, Who Has?: Math • 3–4 © 2006 Creative Teaching Press

Changing Mixed Numbers to Decimals

Directions: As your classmates identify the answers, write each decimal in the grid from left to right and top to bottom.

Yellow →											
Purple											
Blue											
Green											8.8

Write a fraction that equals each decimal in the purple row.

1. _____ = _____

2. _____ = _____

3. _____ = _____

4. _____ = _____

5. _____ = _____

6. _____ = _____

7. _____ = _____

8. _____ = _____

9. _____ = _____

10. _____ = _____

I have the **first card.**

Who has the fraction equal to 1.2?

I have $5\frac{3}{10}$.

Who has the fraction equal to 1.25?

I have $1\frac{2}{10}$.

Who has the fraction equal to 2.99?

I have $1\frac{25}{100}$.

Who has the fraction equal to 2.6?

I have $2\frac{99}{100}$.

Who has the fraction equal to 3.1?

I have $2\frac{6}{10}$.

Who has the fraction equal to 5.19?

I have $3\frac{1}{10}$.

Who has the fraction equal to 4.44?

I have $5\frac{19}{100}$.

Who has the fraction equal to 1.9?

I have $4\frac{44}{100}$.

Who has the fraction equal to 5.3?

I have $1\frac{9}{10}$.

Who has the fraction equal to 6.25?

I Have, Who Has?: Math • 3–4 © 2006 Creative Teaching Press

Changing Decimals to Mixed Numbers

I have **6²⁵/₁₀₀**.

Who has the fraction equal to 2.48?

I have **2⁷/₁₀**.

Who has the fraction equal to 6.81?

I have **2⁴⁸/₁₀₀**.

Who has the fraction equal to 6.9?

I have **6⁸¹/₁₀₀**.

Who has the fraction equal to 1.3?

I have **6⁹/₁₀**.

Who has the fraction equal to 4.2?

I have **1³/₁₀**.

Who has the fraction equal to 3.26?

I have **4²/₁₀**.

Who has the fraction equal to 3.88?

I have **3²⁶/₁₀₀**.

Who has the fraction equal to 5.25?

I have **3⁸⁸/₁₀₀**.

Who has the fraction equal to 2.7?

I have **5²⁵/₁₀₀**.

Who has the fraction equal to 3.7?

Changing Decimals to Mixed Numbers

I have **3⁷/₁₀.**

Who has the fraction equal to 1.72?

I have **6⁴/₁₀.**

Who has the fraction equal to 2.36?

I have **1⁷²/₁₀₀.**

Who has the fraction equal to 4.9?

I have **2³⁶/₁₀₀.**

Who has the fraction equal to 1.4?

I have **4⁹/₁₀.**

Who has the fraction equal to 1.87?

I have **1⁴/₁₀.**

Who has the fraction equal to 4.17?

I have **1⁸⁷/₁₀₀.**

Who has the fraction equal to 5.4?

I have **4¹⁷/₁₀₀.**

Who has the fraction equal to 6.06?

I have **5⁴/₁₀.**

Who has the fraction equal to 6.4?

I have **6⁶/₁₀₀.**

Who has the fraction equal to 1.09?

I Have, Who Has?: Math • 3–4 © 2006 Creative Teaching Press

I have **1⁹/₁₀₀.**

Who has the fraction equal to 4.8?

I have **3³³/₁₀₀.**

Who has the fraction equal to 6.36?

I have **4⁸/₁₀.**

Who has the fraction equal to 6.5?

I have **6³⁶/₁₀₀.**

Who has the fraction equal to 2.03?

I have **6⁵/₁₀.**

Who has the fraction equal to 4.01?

I have **2³/₁₀₀.**

Who has the fraction equal to 2.4?

I have **4¹/₁₀₀.**

Who has the fraction equal to 3.3?

I have **2⁴/₁₀.**

Who has the fraction equal to 3.07?

I have **3³/₁₀.**

Who has the fraction equal to 3.33?

I have **3⁷/₁₀₀.**

Who has the first card?

Changing Decimals to Mixed Numbers

Directions: Complete the maze by highlighting the answers as your classmates identify them.

What did the duck say when she bought lipstick?

$1\frac{9}{10}$ S	$3\frac{3}{10}$ Y	$4\frac{1}{100}$ U	$2\frac{48}{100}$ E	$2\frac{48}{100}$ S	$6\frac{25}{100}$ R	$1\frac{9}{10}$ O
$6\frac{36}{100}$ P	$3\frac{33}{100}$ H	$6\frac{5}{10}$ A	$5\frac{12}{100}$ P	$6\frac{9}{10}$ N	$6\frac{9}{100}$ U	$5\frac{19}{100}$ A
$2\frac{3}{100}$ C	$7\frac{45}{100}$ T	$4\frac{8}{10}$ I	$3\frac{88}{100}$ M	$4\frac{2}{10}$ A	$1\frac{25}{100}$ W	$2\frac{6}{10}$ M
$2\frac{4}{10}$ S	$2\frac{2}{100}$ I	$1\frac{9}{100}$ L	$2\frac{7}{10}$ L	$1\frac{9}{10}$ T	$5\frac{3}{10}$ I	$5\frac{3}{100}$ O
Finish $3\frac{7}{100}$	$4\frac{17}{100}$ B	$6\frac{6}{100}$ A	$6\frac{81}{100}$ W	$6\frac{8}{10}$ N	$4\frac{44}{100}$ E	$4\frac{4}{10}$ M
$8\frac{2}{100}$ Y	$1\frac{4}{10}$ E	$2\frac{36}{100}$ D	$1\frac{3}{10}$ S	$3\frac{1}{100}$ B	$3\frac{1}{10}$ O	$1\frac{25}{100}$ I
$1\frac{25}{100}$ L	$5\frac{4}{10}$ S	$6\frac{4}{10}$ A	$3\frac{26}{100}$ O	$5\frac{25}{100}$ G	$2\frac{99}{100}$ Y	$1\frac{9}{10}$ L
$2\frac{48}{100}$ R	$1\frac{87}{100}$ T	$4\frac{9}{10}$ Y	$1\frac{72}{100}$ H	$3\frac{7}{10}$ I	$1\frac{2}{10}$ O	**Start** *

Follow these directions to reveal the answer to the riddle.

1. Cross out the first fraction you did **not** already highlight in the game.

2. Cross out all the fractions equal to 2.48.

3. Write the letters in the boxes that are **not** highlighted or crossed out on the blanks below. Write the letters in order from left to right and top to bottom.

"____ ____ ____ ____   ____ ____ ____   ____ ____ ____   ____ ____ ____   ____ ____ ____ ____."

Choose five fractions that are **not** highlighted or crossed out. Write them in decimal form on the back of this paper.

I Have, Who Has?: Math • 3–4 © 2006 Creative Teaching Press

Comparing Decimals

I have the **first card.**

Who has the decimal that is greater:
1.9 or 1.3?

I have **2.75.**

Who has the decimal that is smaller:
5.5 or 5.05?

I have **1.9.**

Who has the decimal that is smaller:
2.34 or 2.43?

I have **5.05.**

Who has the decimal that is greater:
3.13 or 3.03?

I have **2.34.**

Who has the decimal that is greater:
4.3 or 4.1?

I have **3.13.**

Who has the decimal that is smaller:
4.25 or 4.52?

I have **4.3.**

Who has the decimal that is smaller:
2.05 or 2.5?

I have **4.25.**

Who has the decimal that is greater:
1.05 or 1.5?

I have **2.05.**

Who has the decimal that is greater:
2.75 or 2.57?

I have **1.5.**

Who has the decimal that is smaller:
2.25 or 2.52?

I Have, Who Has?: Math • 3–4 © 2006 Creative Teaching Press

Comparing Decimals

I have **2.25.**

Who has the decimal that is greater: 3.07 or 3.7?

I have **3.34.**

Who has the decimal that is smaller: 5.5 or 5.25?

I have **3.7.**

Who has the decimal that is smaller: 1.7 or 1.07?

I have **5.25.**

Who has the decimal that is greater: 3.54 or 3.45?

I have **1.07.**

Who has the decimal that is greater: 4.17 or 4.7?

I have **3.54.**

Who has the decimal that is greater: 6.07 or 6.7?

I have **4.7.**

Who has the decimal that is smaller: 4.5 or 4.19?

I have **6.7.**

Who has the decimal that is greater: 5.8 or 5.68?

I have **4.19.**

Who has the decimal that is smaller: 3.34 or 3.43?

I have **5.8.**

Who has the decimal that is smaller: 2.6 or 2.45?

I Have, Who Has?: Math • 3–4 © 2006 Creative Teaching Press

Comparing Decimals

I have **2.45.**

Who has the decimal that is greater:
4.78 or 4.8?

I have **5.7.**

Who has the decimal that is smaller:
3.4 or 3.24?

I have **4.8.**

Who has the decimal that is smaller:
3.7 or 3.67?

I have **3.24.**

Who has the decimal that is greater:
4.04 or 4.4?

I have **3.67.**

Who has the decimal that is greater:
5.4 or 5.39?

I have **4.4.**

Who has the decimal that is smaller:
2.6 or 2.06?

I have **5.4.**

Who has the decimal that is smaller:
4.5 or 4.6?

I have **2.06.**

Who has the decimal that is greater:
3.4 or 3.37?

I have **4.5.**

Who has the decimal that is greater:
5.7 or 5.07?

I have **3.4.**

Who has the decimal that is smaller:
5.09 or 5.9?

 # Comparing Decimals

I have **5.09.**

Who has the decimal that is greater:
4.56 or 4.65?

I have **5.9.**

Who has the decimal that is smaller:
3.99 or 3.9?

I have **4.65.**

Who has the decimal that is smaller:
2.56 or 2.65?

I have **3.9.**

Who has the decimal that is greater:
2.98 or 2.89?

I have **2.56.**

Who has the decimal that is greater:
1.23 or 1.32?

I have **2.98.**

Who has the decimal that is smaller:
0.75 or 1.1?

I have **1.32.**

Who has the decimal that is smaller:
5.6 or 5.06?

I have **0.75.**

Who has the decimal that is greater:
5.5 or 5.3?

I have **5.06.**

Who has the decimal that is greater:
5.59 or 5.9?

I have **5.5.**

Who has the first card?

I Have, Who Has?: Math • 3–4 © 2006 Creative Teaching Press

Comparing Decimals

Directions: As your classmates identify the answers, write each decimal in the grid from left to right and top to bottom.

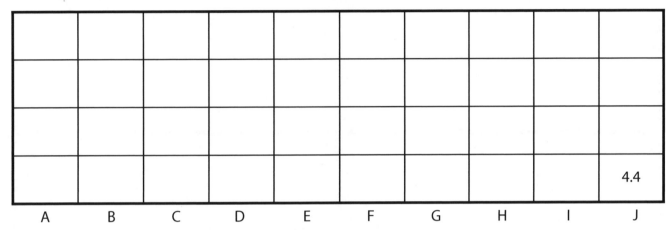

									4.4
A	B	C	D	E	F	G	H	I	J

Write the decimals in each column in order from least to greatest.

A. _____ < _____ < _____ < _____

B. _____ < _____ < _____ < _____

C. _____ < _____ < _____ < _____

D. _____ < _____ < _____ < _____

E. _____ < _____ < _____ < _____

F. _____ < _____ < _____ < _____

G. _____ < _____ < _____ < _____

H. _____ < _____ < _____ < _____

I. _____ < _____ < _____ < _____

J. _____ < _____ < _____ < _____

Comparing Mixed Numbers and Decimals

I have the first card.

Who has the number that is greater: 3.5 or 3⅘?

I have 1.9.

Who has the number that is smaller: 2⅔ or 2.23?

I have 3⅘.

Who has the number that is smaller: 2⅞ or 2.35?

I have 2.23.

Who has the number that is greater: 3.67 or 3⅓?

I have 2.35.

Who has the number that is greater: 5⅘ or 5.299?

I have 3.67.

Who has the number that is smaller: 1.45 or 1¹⁄₁₀?

I have 5⅘.

Who has the number that is smaller: 4.04 or 4³⁄₁₀?

I have 1¹⁄₁₀.

Who has the number that is greater: 2.28 or 2⁸⁄₉?

I have 4.04.

Who has the number that is greater: 1⅚ or 1.9?

I have 2⁸⁄₉.

Who has the number that is smaller: 5.15 or 5¹⁄₁₀?

I Have, Who Has?: Math • 3–4 © 2006 Creative Teaching Press

Comparing Mixed Numbers and Decimals

I have **5¹/₁₀.**

Who has the number that is greater:
3.8 or 3²/₅?

I have **5.49.**

Who has the number that is smaller:
4³/₈ or 4.88?

I have **3.8.**

Who has the number that is smaller:
4.37 or 4⁴/₅?

I have **4³/₈.**

Who has the number that is greater:
3⁷/₉ or 3.97?

I have **4.37.**

Who has the number that is greater:
5.89 or 5⁹/₁₀?

I have **3.97.**

Who has the number that is smaller:
5.5 or 5³/₁₀?

I have **5⁹/₁₀.**

Who has the number that is smaller:
3⁷/₁₀ or 3.37?

I have **5³/₁₀.**

Who has the number that is greater:
4.04 or 4⁴/₁₀?

I have **3.37.**

Who has the number that is greater:
5.49 or 5¹/₉?

I have **4⁴/₁₀.**

Who has the number that is smaller:
5⅓ or 5.81?

I Have, Who Has?: Math • 3–4 © 2006 Creative Teaching Press

I have **5⅓.**

Who has the number that is greater:
3.5 or 3.05?

I have **1⁵⁄₆.**

Who has the number that is smaller:
2.8 or 2⅔?

I have **3.5.**

Who has the number that is smaller:
2.99 or 2⅞?

I have **2⅔.**

Who has the number that is greater:
3⅓ or 3.13?

I have **2⅞.**

Who has the number that is greater:
5⁹⁄₁₀₀ or 5.299?

I have **3⅓.**

Who has the number that is smaller:
1½ or 1.45?

I have **5.299.**

Who has the number that is smaller:
4³⁄₁₀ or 4.5?

I have **1.45.**

Who has the number that is greater:
2¹⁄₁₅ or 2.28?

I have **4³⁄₁₀.**

Who has the number that is greater:
1⅚ or 1.2?

I have **2.28.**

Who has the number that is smaller:
5.15 or 5⅖?

I Have, Who Has?: Math • 3–4 © 2006 Creative Teaching Press

Comparing Mixed Numbers and Decimals

I have **5.15.**

Who has the number that is greater:
3.05 or 3²⁄₅?

I have **5¹⁄₉.**

Who has the number that is smaller:
4⁹⁄₁₀ or 4.88?

I have **3²⁄₅.**

Who has the number that is smaller:
4.91 or 4⁴⁄₅?

I have **4.88.**

Who has the number that is greater:
3.17 or 3⁷⁄₉?

I have **4⁴⁄₅.**

Who has the number that is greater:
5⁸⁄₁₀ or 5.89?

I have **3⁷⁄₉.**

Who has the number that is smaller:
5.5 or 5.55?

I have **5.89.**

Who has the number that is smaller:
3⁷⁄₁₀ or 3.89?

I have **5.5.**

Who has the number that is greater:
5⁸⁄₁₀ or 5.81?

I have **3⁷⁄₁₀.**

Who has the number that is greater:
5¹⁄₉ or 5.09?

I have **5.81.**

Who has the first card?

I Have, Who Has?: Math • 3–4 © 2006 Creative Teaching Press

Comparing Mixed Numbers and Decimals

Directions: Complete the maze by highlighting the answers as your classmates identify them.

What kind of mistakes do spooks make?

5³⁄₁₀	T	5⁹⁄₁₀	H	1⁵⁄₆	E	3.67	E	1¹⁄₁₀	P
5.49	Y	3.5	M	2⁷⁄₈	A	2.23	F	2⁸⁄₉	A
2.35	B	5⁴⁄₅	U	4.04	M	1.9	Q	5¹⁄₁₀	I
3⁴⁄₅	N	1¹⁄₁₀	K	4.88	E	4.37	A	3.8	W
Start *		1⁵⁄₆	B	1.45	O	5⁹⁄₁₀	C	3.37	D
5⁹⁄₁₀	O	3⁷⁄₁₀	S	5.89	S	4⁴⁄₅	T	5.49	A
4.88	S	5¹⁄₉	B	5.15	E	3²⁄₅	L	4³⁄₈	R
3⁷⁄₉	C	3.67	B	2.28	U	2.35	O	3.97	F
5.5	M	3¹⁄₃	O	1.45	T	4⁴⁄₁₀	S	5³⁄₁₀	D
Finish 5.81		2²⁄₃	P	3.67	O	5¹⁄₃	R	3.5	Y
5³⁄₁₀	S	1⁵⁄₆	Y	4³⁄₁₀	A	5.299	H	2⁷⁄₈	H

Write the letters that are **not** highlighted on the blanks below to reveal the answer to the riddle. Write the letters in order from left to right and top to bottom.

____ ____ ____ ____   ____ ____ ____   ____ ____ ____ - ____ ____ ____ ____.

Write the first four fractions and/or decimals that are **not** highlighted or crossed out. Write these fractions in the middle column. Write a fraction that is smaller and greater than each fraction.

1. _____ < _____ < _____

2. _____ < _____ < _____

3. _____ < _____ < _____

4. _____ < _____ < _____

I Have, Who Has?: Math • 3–4 © 2006 Creative Teaching Press

I have the **first card.**

Who has the next number in this pattern: 20, 40, 60, 80, ____?

I have **9.**

Who has the next number in this pattern: 44, 55, 66, ____?

I have **100.**

Who has the next number in this pattern: 6, 12, 18, _____?

I have **77.**

Who has the next number in this pattern: 30, 40, 50, _____?

I have **24.**

Who has the next number in this pattern: 5, 10, 15, _____?

I have **60.**

Who has the next number in this pattern: 52, 54, 56, _____?

I have **20.**

Who has the next number in this pattern: 2, 4, 6, _____?

I have **58.**

Who has the next number in this pattern: 10, 13, 16, 19, ____?

I have **8.**

Who has the next number in this pattern: 3, 5, 7, _____?

I have **22.**

Who has the next number in this pattern: 13, 23, 33, 43, _____?

I Have, Who Has?: Math • 3–4 © 2006 Creative Teaching Press

Number Patterns—Addition and Multiplication

I have **53.**

Who has the next number in this pattern: 30, 60, 90, _____?

I have **82.**

Who has the next number in this pattern: 2, 4, 8, 16, 32, _____?

I have **120.**

Who has the next number in this pattern: 7, 17, 27, _____?

I have **64.**

Who has the next number in this pattern: 3, 8, 13, 18, 23, _____?

I have **37.**

Who has the next number in this pattern: 9, 18, 27, 36, _____?

I have **28.**

Who has the next number in this pattern: 3, 6, 12, 24, 48, _____?

I have **45.**

Who has the next number in this pattern: 15, 20, 25, _____?

I have **96.**

Who has the next number in this pattern: 15, 30, 45, 60, _____?

I have **30.**

Who has the next number in this pattern: 52, 62, 72, _____?

I have **75.**

Who has the next number in this pattern: 32, 42, 52, _____?

I Have, Who Has?: Math • 3–4 © 2006 Creative Teaching Press

I have **62.**

Who has the next number in this pattern: 18, 20, 22, 24, _____?

I have **7.**

Who has the next number in this pattern: 1, 12, 23, 34, 45, ___?

I have **26.**

Who has the next number in this pattern: 33, 44, 55, _____?

I have **56.**

Who has the next number in this pattern: 8, 16, 24, _____?

I have **66.**

Who has the next number in this pattern: 41, 51, 61, _____?

I have **32.**

Who has the next number in this pattern: 12, 24, 36, _____?

I have **71.**

Who has the next number in this pattern: 11, 13, 15, 17, _____?

I have **48.**

Who has the next number in this pattern: 34, 54, 74, _____?

I have **19.**

Who has the next number in this pattern: 1, 3, 5, _____?

I have **94.**

Who has the next number in the pattern: 14, 21, 28, _____?

I have **35.**

Who has the next number in this
pattern: 55, 66, 77, _____?

I have **44.**

Who has the next number in this
pattern: 75, 78, 81, 84, _____?

I have **88.**

Who has the next number in this
pattern: 53, 63, 73, _____?

I have **87.**

Who has the next number in this
pattern: 42, 44, 46, 48, _____?

I have **83.**

Who has the next number in this
pattern: 20, 24, 28, 32, _____?

I have **50.**

Who has the next number in this
pattern: 28, 35, 42, _____?

I have **36.**

Who has the next number in this
pattern: 4, 15, 26, 37, 48, _____?

I have **49.**

Who has the next number in this
pattern: 1, 12, 23, _____?

I have **59.**

Who has the next number in this
pattern: 11, 22, 33, _____?

I have **34.**

Who has the first card?

I Have, Who Has?: Math • 3–4 © 2006 Creative Teaching Press

Number Patterns—Addition and Multiplication

Directions: Highlight the answers as your classmates identify them.

1	2	3	4	5	6	7	8	9	10
11	12	13	14	15	16	17	18	19	20
21	22	23	24	25	26	27	28	29	30
31	32	33	34	35	36	37	38	39	40
41	42	43	44	45	46	47	48	49	50
51	52	53	54	55	56	57	58	59	60
61	62	63	64	65	66	67	68	69	70
71	72	73	74	75	76	77	78	79	80
81	82	83	84	85	86	87	88	89	90
91	92	93	94	95	96	97	98	99	100
101	102	103	104	105	106	107	108	109	110
111	112	113	114	115	116	117	118	119	120
A	B	C	D	E	F	G	H	I	J

Write an addition or a multiplication number pattern for each number **not** highlighted in Column B.

1. _____

2. _____

3. _____

4. _____

5. _____

6. _____

7. _____

8. _____

I have the first card.

Who has the next number in this pattern: 80, 60, 40, _____?

I have 19.

Who has the next number in this pattern: 48, 36, 24, _____?

I have 20.

Who has the next number in this pattern: 98, 96, 94, _____?

I have 12.

Who has the next number in this pattern: 41, 31, 21, _____?

I have 92.

Who has the next number in this pattern: 77, 67, 57, _____?

I have 11.

Who has the next number in this pattern: 88, 77, 66, _____?

I have 47.

Who has the next number in this pattern: 25, 20, 15, _____?

I have 55.

Who has the next number in this pattern: 120, 108, 96, 84, _____?

I have 10.

Who has the next number in this pattern: 79, 59, 39, _____?

I have 72.

Who has the next number in this pattern: 100, 75, 50, _____?

I have **25.**

Who has the next number in this pattern: 60, 45, 30, _____?

I have **23.**

Who has the next number in this pattern: 60, 48, 36, _____?

I have **15.**

Who has the next number in this pattern: 28, 21, 14, _____?

I have **24.**

Who has the next number in this pattern: 6, 5, 4, 3, _____?

I have **7.**

Who has the next number in this pattern: 36, 30, 24, _____?

I have **2.**

Who has the next number in this pattern: 66, 55, 44, _____?

I have **18.**

Who has the next number in this pattern: 71, 61, 51, _____?

I have **33.**

Who has the next number in this pattern: 40, 32, 24, 16, _____?

I have **41.**

Who has the next number in this pattern: 56, 45, 34, _____?

I have **8.**

Who has the next number in this pattern: 40, 20, 10, _____?

I have **5.**

Who has the next number in this pattern: 30, 27, 24, _____?

I have **50.**

Who has the next number in this pattern: 89, 69, 49, _____?

I have **21.**

Who has the next number in this pattern: 67, 56, 45, _____?

I have **29.**

Who has the next number in this pattern: 64, 55, 46, 37, _____?

I have **34.**

Who has the next number in this pattern: 52, 39, 26, _____?

I have **28.**

Who has the next number in this pattern: 60, 55, 50, _____?

I have **13.**

Who has the next number in this pattern: 54, 48, 42, _____?

I have **45.**

Who has the next number in this pattern: 64, 32, 16, 8, _____?

I have **36.**

Who has the next number in this pattern: 95, 80, 65, _____?

I have **4.**

Who has the next number in this pattern: 96, 48, 24, 12, _____?

I Have, Who Has?, Math • 3–4 © 2006 Creative Teaching Press

I have **6.**

Who has the next number in this pattern: 81, 27, 9, _____?

I have **22.**

Who has the next number in this pattern: 240, 180, 120, _____?

I have **3.**

Who has the next number in this pattern: 66, 77, 88, _____?

I have **60.**

Who has the next number in this pattern: 92, 91, 90, _____?

I have **99.**

Who has the next number in this pattern: 72, 36, 18, _____?

I have **89.**

Who has the next number in this pattern: 99, 87, 75, _____?

I have **9.**

Who has the next number in this pattern: 49, 38, 27, _____?

I have **63.**

Who has the next number in this pattern: 86, 80, 74, _____?

I have **16.**

Who has the next number in this pattern: 82, 62, 42, _____?

I have **68.**

Who has the first card?

Number Patterns—Subtraction and Division

Directions: As your classmates identify the answers, write each number in the grid from left to right and top to bottom.

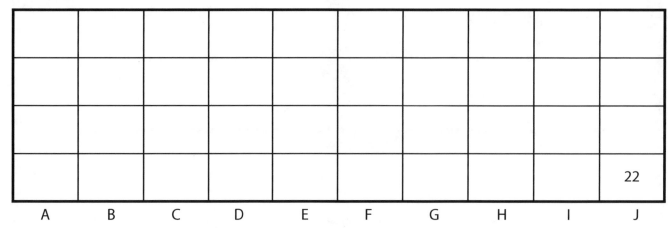

A	B	C	D	E	F	G	H	I	J
									22

Write a subtraction or a division number pattern for each number in columns B, D, and H. The first one is done for you.

1. _____124_____, _____116_____, _____108_____, _____100_____, _____92_____

2. _____, _____, _____, _____, _____

3. _____, _____, _____, _____, _____

4. _____, _____, _____, _____, _____

5. _____, _____, _____, _____, _____

6. _____, _____, _____, _____, _____

7. _____, _____, _____, _____, _____

8. _____, _____, _____, _____, _____

9. _____, _____, _____, _____, _____

10. _____, _____, _____, _____, _____

11. _____, _____, _____, _____, _____

12. _____, _____, _____, _____, _____

I Have, Who Has?: Math • 3–4 © 2006 Creative Teaching Press

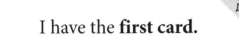

I have the **first card.**

Who has the next number in this pattern: 15, 30, 45, _____?

I have **45.**

Who has the next number in this pattern: 14, 21, 28, _____?

I have **60.**

Who has the next number in this pattern: 77, 66, 55, _____?

I have **35.**

Who has the next number in this pattern: 400, 200, 100, _____?

I have **44.**

Who has the next number in this pattern: 25, 50, 75, _____?

I have **50.**

Who has the next number in this pattern: 7, 14, 28, _____?

I have **100.**

Who has the next number in this pattern: 100, 80, 60, _____?

I have **56.**

Who has the next number in this pattern: 55, 44, 33, _____?

I have **40.**

Who has the next number in this pattern: 54, 51, 48, _____?

I have **22.**

Who has the next number in the pattern: 75, 60, 45, _____?

Number Patterns—All Operations

I have **30.**

Who has the next number in this
pattern: 97, 77, 57, _____?

I have **72.**

Who has the next number in this
pattern: 67, 64, 61, _____?

I have **37.**

Who has the next number in this
pattern: 23, 43, 63, _____?

I have **58.**

Who has the next number in this
pattern: 85, 74, 63, _____?

I have **83.**

Who has the next number in this
pattern: 625, 125, 25, _____?

I have **52.**

Who has the next number in this
pattern: 20, 16, 12, 8, _____?

I have **5.**

Who has the next number in this
pattern: 60, 45, 30, _____?

I have **4.**

Who has the next number in this
pattern: 83, 63, 43, _____?

I have **15.**

Who has the next number in this
pattern: 36, 48, 60, _____?

I have **23.**

Who has the next number in this
pattern: 60, 48, 36, _____?

I Have, Who Has?: Math • 3–4 © 2006 Creative Teaching Press

I have **24.**

Who has the next number in this pattern: 13, 15, 17, _____?

I have **2.**

Who has the next number in this pattern: 44, 33, 22, _____?

I have **19.**

Who has the next number in this pattern: 280, 210, 140, _____?

I have **11.**

Who has the next number in this pattern: 80, 60, 40, _____?

I have **70.**

Who has the next number in this pattern: 84, 82, 80, _____?

I have **20.**

Who has the next number in this pattern: 9, 18, 27, _____?

I have **78.**

Who has the next number in this pattern: 93, 73, 53, _____?

I have **36.**

Who has the next number in this pattern: 100, 75, 50, _____?

I have **33.**

Who has the next number in this pattern: 54, 18, 6, _____?

I have **25.**

Who has the next number in this pattern: 33, 55, 77, _____?

I have **99.**

Who has the next number in this pattern: 66, 76, 86, _____?

I have **63.**

Who has the next number in this pattern: 40, 48, 56, _____?

I have **96.**

Who has the next number in this pattern: 25, 45, 65, _____?

I have **64.**

Who has the next number in this pattern: 91, 71, 51, _____?

I have **85.**

Who has the next number in this pattern: 81, 72, 63, _____?

I have **31.**

Who has the next number in this pattern: 48, 60, 72, _____?

I have **54.**

Who has the next number in this pattern: 99, 88, 77, _____?

I have **84.**

Who has the next number in this pattern: 92, 90, 88, _____?

I have **66.**

Who has the next number in this pattern: 42, 49, 56, _____?

I have **86.**

Who has the first card?

I Have, Who Has?: Math • 3–4 © 2006 Creative Teaching Press

Number Patterns—All Operations

Directions: Complete the maze by highlighting the answers as your classmates identify them.

What did the postcard say to the stamp?

Start *																				
60	A	44	L	22	K	31	S	20	S	56	P	22	M	16	T	30	V
45	C	14	T	100	O	40	D	45	P	35	G	50	N	30	S	37	Y	12	B
76	I	28	C	33	J	78	N	51	K	38	X	42	W	88	I	83	Z	6	T
32	H	70	M	2	C	70	I	23	R	4	F	72	M	15	Q	5	G	38	E
44	B	33	A	11	I	19	U	24	B	52	Q	58	E	8	N	59	M	**Finish** 86	F
62	D	48	W	20	W	10	O	18	D	85	W	54	J	64	T	31	H	84	P
90	E	47	W	36	L	25	X	99	V	96	U	66	Z	63	R	3	I	50	L
100	L	25	G	86	O	82	P	80	L	7	A	23	C	75	E	26	O	37	S

Follow these directions to reveal the answer to the riddle.

- Identify the number that comes next in each pattern below.

- Cross out these numbers in the grid above.

- Write the letters that are **not** highlighted or crossed out on the blanks below. Write the letters in order from left to right and top to bottom.

1. 52, 42, 32, _____

2. 5, 10, 15, _____

3. 4, 8, 12, _____

4. 75, 60, 45, _____

5. 18, 27, 36, _____

6. 48, 36, 24, _____

7. 98, 78, 58, _____

8. 32, 36, 40, _____

9. 89, 79, 69, _____

10. 25, 20, 15, _____

11. 45, 36, 27, _____

12. 56, 46, 36, _____

" ___ ___ ___ ___ ___ ___   ___ ___ ___ ___   ___ ___ ___ ___ ___   ___ ___ ___   ___ ___

___ ___ ___ ___ ___   ___ ___ ___   ___ ___ ___ ___ ___ ___ ___!"

I Have, Who Has?: Math • 3–4 © 2006 Creative Teaching Press

Solve for n 1

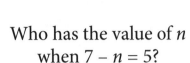

I have the **first card.**

Who has the value of n
when $7 - n = 5$?

I have **12.**

Who has the value of n
when $9 + n = 20$?

I have **2.**

Who has the value of n
when $12 + n = 20$?

I have **11.**

Who has the value of n
when $n \div 11 = 3$?

I have **8.**

Who has the value of n
when $15 - n = 6$?

I have **33.**

Who has the value of n
when $35 - n = 3$?

I have **9.**

Who has the value of n
when $2 \times n = 50$?

I have **32.**

Who has the value of n
when $n + 50 = 90$?

I have **25.**

Who has the value of n
when $144 \div n = 12$?

I have **40.**

Who has the value of n
when $25 \times n = 75$?

I Have, Who Has?: Math • 3–4 © 2006 Creative Teaching Press

Solve for n 1

I have **3.**

Who has the value of n
when $n \div 5 = 11$?

I have **15.**

Who has the value of n
when $40 - n = 9$?

I have **55.**

Who has the value of n
when $n \div 5 = 7$?

I have **31.**

Who has the value of n
when $54 \div n = 9$?

I have **35.**

Who has the value of n
when $9 \times 2 = n$?

I have **6.**

Who has the value of n
when $n \times 9 = 63$?

I have **18.**

Who has the value of n
when $60 \div n = 12$?

I have **7.**

Who has the value of n
when $100 \div n = 10$?

I have **5.**

Who has the value of n
when $n \times 2 = 30$?

I have **10.**

Who has the value of n
when ½ of $n = 30$?

I have **60.**

Who has the value of *n*
when *n* ÷ 4 = 11?

I have **20.**

Who has the value of *n*
when 100 − *n* = 30?

I have **44.**

Who has the value of *n*
when *n* − 75 = 25?

I have **70.**

Who has the value of *n*
when ½ of *n* = 40?

I have **100.**

Who has the value of *n*
when *n* ÷ 8 = 9?

I have **80.**

Who has the value of *n*
when *n* + 12 = 64?

I have **72.**

Who has the value of *n*
when 2 × *n* = 44?

I have **52.**

Who has the value of *n*
when 3 × *n* = 90?

I have **22.**

Who has the value of *n*
when 5 × *n* = 100?

I have **30.**

Who has the value of *n*
when 61 − *n* = 11?

I Have, Who Has?: Math • 3–4 © 2006 Creative Teaching Press

I have **50.**

Who has the value of n
when $n \div 7 = 7$?

I have **45.**

Who has the value of n
when $n \div 9 = 3$?

I have **49.**

Who has the value of n
when $48 \div n = 12$?

I have **27.**

Who has the value of n
when $n \times 2 = 28$?

I have **4.**

Who has the value of n
when $17 + n = 30$?

I have **14.**

Who has the value of n
when $n \times 2 = 32$?

I have **13.**

Who has the value of n
when $n + 9 = 50$?

I have **16.**

Who has the value of n
when $30 - n = 7$?

I have **41.**

Who has the value of n
when $n \div 5 = 9$?

I have **23.**

Who has the first card?

Solve for n 1

Directions: Highlight the answers as your classmates identify them.

1	2	3	4	5	6	7	8	9	10
11	12	13	14	15	16	17	18	19	20
21	22	23	24	25	26	27	28	29	30
31	32	33	34	35	36	37	38	39	40
41	42	43	44	45	46	47	48	49	50
51	52	53	54	55	56	57	58	59	60
61	62	63	64	65	66	67	68	69	70
71	72	73	74	75	76	77	78	79	80
81	82	83	84	85	86	87	88	89	90
91	92	93	94	95	96	97	98	99	100
A	B	C	D	E	F	G	H	I	J

Write algebraic equations in terms of *n* for all of the numbers **not** highlighted in columns B and E. The first one is done for you.

1. $n = \underline{\quad 2 \quad}$ in my equation $\underline{\qquad\qquad 21 \times n \qquad\qquad}$ = $\underline{\qquad 42 \qquad}$

2. $n = \underline{\qquad}$ in my equation $\underline{\qquad\qquad\qquad\qquad\qquad\qquad}$ = $\underline{\qquad\qquad\qquad}$

3. $n = \underline{\qquad}$ in my equation $\underline{\qquad\qquad\qquad\qquad\qquad\qquad}$ = $\underline{\qquad\qquad\qquad}$

4. $n = \underline{\qquad}$ in my equation $\underline{\qquad\qquad\qquad\qquad\qquad\qquad}$ = $\underline{\qquad\qquad\qquad}$

5. $n = \underline{\qquad}$ in my equation $\underline{\qquad\qquad\qquad\qquad\qquad\qquad}$ = $\underline{\qquad\qquad\qquad}$

6. $n = \underline{\qquad}$ in my equation $\underline{\qquad\qquad\qquad\qquad\qquad\qquad}$ = $\underline{\qquad\qquad\qquad}$

7. $n = \underline{\qquad}$ in my equation $\underline{\qquad\qquad\qquad\qquad\qquad\qquad}$ = $\underline{\qquad\qquad\qquad}$

8. $n = \underline{\qquad}$ in my equation $\underline{\qquad\qquad\qquad\qquad\qquad\qquad}$ = $\underline{\qquad\qquad\qquad}$

Solve for n 2

I have the **first card.**

Who has the value of n
when $100 \div n = 4$?

I have **15.**

Who has the value of n
when $36 \div n = 3$?

I have **25.**

Who has the value of n
when $3 \times n = 27$?

I have **12.**

Who has the value of n
when $121 \div n = 11$?

I have **9.**

Who has the value of n
when $40 + n = 68$?

I have **11.**

Who has the value of n
when $n - 25 = 26$?

I have **28.**

Who has the value of n
when $n \div 8 = 4$?

I have **51.**

Who has the value of n
when $100 - n = 20$?

I have **32.**

Who has the value of n
when $n \times 3 = 45$?

I have **80.**

Who has the value of n
when $n \div 6 = 9$?

Solve for n 2

I have **54.**

Who has the value of n
when $2 \times n = 88$?

I have **56.**

Who has the value of n
when $n \div 9 = 7$?

I have **44.**

Who has the value of n
when $4 \times n = 88$?

I have **63.**

Who has the value of n
when $100 \div n = 10$?

I have **22.**

Who has the value of n
when $5 \times n = 100$?

I have **10.**

Who has the value of n
when $12 \times n = 96$?

I have **20.**

Who has the value of n
when $75 \div n = 25$?

I have **8.**

Who has the value of n
when $n \times 2 = 28$?

I have **3.**

Who has the value of n
when $n \div 7 = 8$?

I have **14.**

Who has the value of n
when $75 - n = 20$?

I Have, Who Has?: Math • 3–4 © 2006 Creative Teaching Press

I have **55.**

Who has the value of n
when $n \div 7 = 7$?

I have **6.**

Who has the value of n
when $100 - n = 1$?

I have **49.**

Who has the value of n
when $n \times 2 = 90$?

I have **99.**

Who has the value of n
when $50 + n = 88$?

I have **45.**

Who has the value of n
when $n \times 3 = 99$?

I have **38.**

Who has the value of n
when $n \times 2 = 48$?

I have **33.**

Who has the value of n
when ½ of $n = 50$?

I have **24.**

Who has the value of n
when $n - 18 = 30$?

I have **100.**

Who has the value of n
when $72 \div n = 12$?

I have **48.**

Who has the value of n
when $n - 27 = 50$?

Solve for n 2

I have **77.** Who has the value of n when $n \div 3 = 12$?	I have **16.** Who has the value of n when $n + 9 = 30$?
I have **36.** Who has the value of n when $9 \times n = 45$?	I have **21.** Who has the value of n when $77 \div n = 11$?
I have **5.** Who has the value of n when $100 - n = 12$?	I have **7.** Who has the value of n when $32 \div n = 8$?
I have **88.** Who has the value of n when $2 \times n = 100$?	I have **4.** Who has the value of n when $25 \times n = 50$?
I have **50.** Who has the value of n when $n \div 4 = 4$?	I have **2.** Who has the first card?

I Have, Who Has?: Math • 3–4 © 2006 Creative Teaching Press

Solve for n 2

Directions: As your classmates identify the answers, write each number in the grid from left to right and top to bottom.

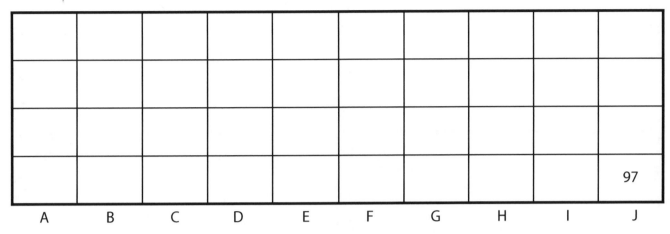

Write algebraic equations in terms of *n* for all of the numbers in columns A, C, and H. The first one is done for you.

1. $n = \underline{\quad 4 \quad}$ in my equation $\underline{\hspace{5cm} 100 \div n \hspace{5cm}} = \underline{\quad 25 \quad}$

2. $n = \underline{\hspace{2cm}}$ in my equation $\underline{\hspace{11cm}} = \underline{\hspace{3cm}}$

3. $n = \underline{\hspace{2cm}}$ in my equation $\underline{\hspace{11cm}} = \underline{\hspace{3cm}}$

4. $n = \underline{\hspace{2cm}}$ in my equation $\underline{\hspace{11cm}} = \underline{\hspace{3cm}}$

5. $n = \underline{\hspace{2cm}}$ in my equation $\underline{\hspace{11cm}} = \underline{\hspace{3cm}}$

6. $n = \underline{\hspace{2cm}}$ in my equation $\underline{\hspace{11cm}} = \underline{\hspace{3cm}}$

7. $n = \underline{\hspace{2cm}}$ in my equation $\underline{\hspace{11cm}} = \underline{\hspace{3cm}}$

8. $n = \underline{\hspace{2cm}}$ in my equation $\underline{\hspace{11cm}} = \underline{\hspace{3cm}}$

9. $n = \underline{\hspace{2cm}}$ in my equation $\underline{\hspace{11cm}} = \underline{\hspace{3cm}}$

10. $n = \underline{\hspace{2cm}}$ in my equation $\underline{\hspace{11cm}} = \underline{\hspace{3cm}}$

11. $n = \underline{\hspace{2cm}}$ in my equation $\underline{\hspace{11cm}} = \underline{\hspace{3cm}}$

12. $n = \underline{\hspace{2cm}}$ in my equation $\underline{\hspace{11cm}} = \underline{\hspace{3cm}}$

Solve for n 3

I have the **first card.**

Who has the value of n
when $4 \times n = 48$?

I have **70.**

Who has the value of n
when $8 \times n = 80$?

I have **12.**

Who has the value of n
when $3 \times n = 66$?

I have **10.**

Who has the value of n
when $8 \times n = 56$?

I have **22.**

Who has the value of n
when $n - 3 = 50$?

I have **7.**

Who has the value of n
when $3 \times n = 45$?

I have **53.**

Who has the value of n
when $n + 13 = 75$?

I have **15.**

Who has the value of n
when $12 \times n = 24$?

I have **62.**

Who has the value of n
when $100 - n = 30$?

I have **2.**

Who has the value of n
when $100 - n = 25$?

I Have, Who Has?: Math • 3–4 © 2006 Creative Teaching Press

Solve for n 3

I have **75.**

Who has the value of n
when $n + 2 = 75$?

I have **50.**

Who has the value of n
when $11 + n = 50$?

I have **73.**

Who has the value of n
when $n \div 9 = 9$?

I have **39.**

Who has the value of n
when $n \div 5 = 9$?

I have **81.**

Who has the value of n
when $n \div 4 = 7$?

I have **45.**

Who has the value of n
when $n + 12 = 100$?

I have **28.**

Who has the value of n
when $n + 1 = 27$?

I have **88.**

Who has the value of n
when $n - 2 = 55$?

I have **26.**

Who has the value of n
when $3 \times n = 150$?

I have **57.**

Who has the value of n
when $n - 17 = 50$?

Solve for n 3

I have **67.**

Who has the value of n when $30 \div n = 5$?

I have **17.**

Who has the value of n when $6 \times n = 48$?

I have **6.**

Who has the value of n when $60 \div n = 12$?

I have **8.**

Who has the value of n when $100 - n = 60$?

I have **5.**

Who has the value of n when $n \times 9 = 99$?

I have **40.**

Who has the value of n when $n \times 2 = 62$?

I have **11.**

Who has the value of n when $n - 11 = 50$?

I have **31.**

Who has the value of n when $36 \div n = 9$?

I have **61.**

Who has the value of n when $13 + n = 30$?

I have **4.**

Who has the value of n when $n \div 3 = 7$?

I Have, Who Has?: Math • 3–4 © 2006 Creative Teaching Press

I have **21.**

Who has the value of n
when $n + 12 = 25$?

I have **18.**

Who has the value of n
when $n \div 3 = 9$?

I have **13.**

Who has the value of n
when $24 \div n = 8$?

I have **27.**

Who has the value of n
when $n \div 5 = 5$?

I have **3.**

Who has the value of n
when $n \div 2 = 7$?

I have **25.**

Who has the value of n
when $100 - n = 51$?

I have **14.**

Who has the value of n
when $n \div 2 = 8$?

I have **49.**

Who has the value of n
when $n \div 7 = 6$?

I have **16.**

Who has the value of n
when $n \div 2 = 9$?

I have **42.**

Who has the first card?

Solve for n 3

Directions: As your classmates identify the answers, write the numbers in the grid. Write the first number in the box to the right of "Start" and continue filling in the boxes in a clockwise pattern.

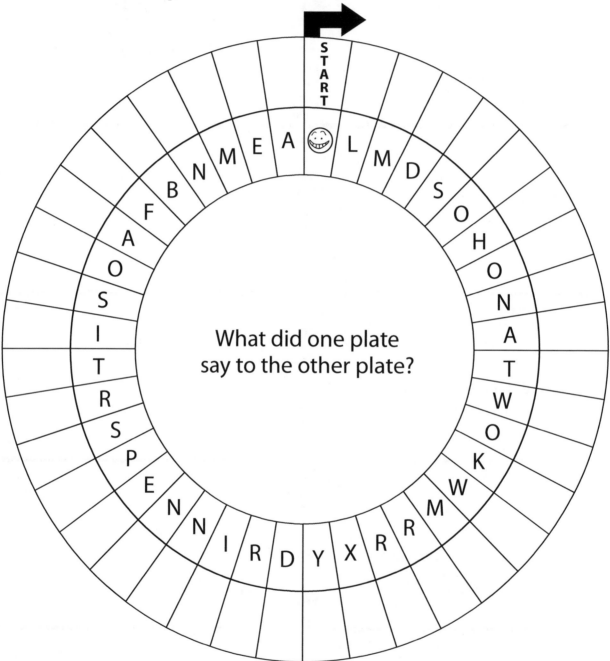

What did one plate say to the other plate?

Cross out the **even** numbers and the matching letters. Write the remaining letters in order on the blanks below to reveal the answer to the riddle.

"____ ____ ____ ____ ____ , ____ ____ ____ ____ ____ ____ ____ . ____ ____ ____ ____ ____ ____ ____ ____

____ ____ ____ ____ ____ ____ ____ !"

I Have, Who Has?: Math • 3–4 © 2006 Creative Teaching Press

Geometry

I have the **first card.**

Who has the word that names a part of a line that has one endpoint?

I have **intersecting lines.**

Who has the type of lines that never touch and are always equally distant at all points from each other?

I have a **ray.**

Who has the name for what is created when two rays share an endpoint?

I have **parallel lines.**

Who has the type of angle that measures less than 90 degrees?

I have an **angle.**

Who has the type of angle that measures exactly 90 degrees?

I have an **acute angle.**

Who has the word that describes two figures that are the same size and shape?

I have a **right angle.**

Who has the type of angle that measures more than 90 degrees?

I have **congruent.**

Who has the word that describes two intersecting lines that create right angles?

I have an **obtuse angle.**

Who has the word that names the type of lines that cross each other?

I have **perpendicular lines.**

Who has the name of the plane figure that has only three angles?

Geometry

I have a **triangle.**

Who has the solid that identifies a ball?

I have a **parallelogram.**

Who has the type of triangle that has sides of different lengths?

I have a **sphere.**

Who has the name for the triangle that has three equal sides?

I have a **scalene triangle.**

Who has the name of a line segment from the center of a circle to any point on the circle?

I have an **equilateral triangle.**

Who has the word that names a figure with four sides?

I have the **radius.**

Who has the line segment that passes through the center of a circle with two endpoints on the circle?

I have a **quadrilateral.**

Who has the type of triangle that has exactly two equal sides and looks like a party hat?

I have the **diameter.**

Who has the polygon with five sides?

I have an **isosceles triangle.**

Who has the name of the figure that is a quadrilateral with two pairs of parallel sides?

I have a **pentagon.**

Who has the polygon with six sides?

I Have, Who Has?: Math • 3–4 © 2006 Creative Teaching Press

Geometry

I have a **hexagon.**

Who has the diameter of a circle if the radius is 3 centimeters?

I have **180.**

Who has the word that describes lines that form from side to side?

I have **6 centimeters.**

Who has the polygon with eight sides?

I have **horizontal.**

Who has the radius of a circular table if the diameter is 13 inches?

I have an **octagon.**

Who has the radius of a circle if the diameter is 9 centimeters?

I have **6.5 inches.**

Who has the diameter of a round placemat if the radius is 5.25 inches?

I have **4.5 centimeters.**

Who has the word that describes lines that form up and down?

I have **10.5 inches.**

Who has the word that names a straight path of points that never stops?

I have **vertical.**

Who has the number of degrees in a line?

I have a **line.**

Who has the measurement of the missing side of an equilateral triangle with the other sides each measuring 7.25 inches?

Geometry

I have **7.25 inches.**

Who has the diameter of a circle with a radius of 1.75 inches?

I have **less than 90 degrees.**

Who has the measurement of an obtuse angle?

I have **3.5 inches.**

Who has the radius of a circle with a diameter of 26 inches?

I have **more than 90 degrees.**

Who has the most likely measurement of the missing side of a scalene triangle measuring 4 inches and 5 inches on the other sides?

I have **13 inches.**

Who has the name of the quadrilateral figure that has one pair of parallel sides?

I have **7 inches.**

Who has the number of sides on a pentagon?

I have a **trapezoid.**

Who has the term that describes an object that is the same on both sides?

I have **five.**

Who has the number of quadrants in a coordinate plane?

I have **symmetrical.**

Who has the measurement of an acute angle?

I have **four.**

Who has the first card?

I Have, Who Has?: Math • 3–4 © 2006 Creative Teaching Press

Geometry

Directions: Complete the maze by highlighting the answers as your classmates identify them.

What do you call an adorable angle?

L trapezoid	M 13 inches	I obtuse angle	T perimeter
R symmetrical	E 3.5 inches	S 7.25 inches	I 7.5 inches
B less than 90 degrees	H more than 90 degrees	N line	S parallel lines
N five	A 7 inches	C 10.5 inches	R 6.5 inches
Finish four	M octagon	Y 4.5 centimeters	I horizontal
O hexagon	S 6 centimeters	U vertical	T 180º
M pentagon	E diameter	A horizontal	N 90º
A right angle	R radius	C trapezoid	U right angle
T line	I scalene triangle	O parallelogram	T isosceles triangle
E 15 inches	A symmetrical	N area	E quadrilateral
P intersecting lines	L parallel lines	A acute angle	R equilateral triangle
W obtuse angle	I right angle	M congruent	T sphere
G octagon	C angle	R perpendicular lines	K triangle
Start*	B ray	L parallelogram	E hexagon

Write the letters that are **not** highlighted on the blanks below to reveal the answer to the riddle.

_____ _____   _____   _____   _____ .

1. Draw the answer to the riddle. Label the degrees.

2. Draw examples of the other two angles. Label the degrees.

I Have, Who Has? Math • 3–4 © 2006 Creative Teaching Press

Money

I have the **first card.**

Who has the total value of two dollars, three quarters, and one dime?

I have **$3.65.**

Who has the total value of six dimes, three nickels, and four pennies?

I have **$2.85.**

Who has the change you would receive if you paid $1.00 for three bags of gumballs at $0.25 each?

I have **$0.79.**

Who has the total value of three dimes, six nickels, and two pennies?

I have **$0.25.**

Who has the total value of five nickels and one quarter?

I have **$0.62.**

Who has the change you would receive after paying $2.00 for a slice of pizza that totaled $1.76?

I have **$0.50.**

Who has the total value of three quarters, two dimes, and one penny?

I have **$0.24.**

Who has the total value of eight nickels and six pennies?

I have **$0.96.**

Who has the change you would receive after buying a $1.35 ice-cream cone with a five-dollar bill?

I have **$0.46.**

Who has the total value of one quarter, two dimes, and four pennies?

I Have, Who Has?: Math • 3–4 © 2006 Creative Teaching Press

Money

I have **$0.49.**

Who has the change you would receive after paying $2.71 for strawberries with a five-dollar bill?

I have **$1.75.**

Who has the total value of five quarters, three dimes, and seven pennies?

I have **$2.29.**

Who has the total value of one five-dollar bill, two quarters, and one nickel?

I have **$1.62.**

Who has the total value of seven quarters, five nickels, and two pennies?

I have **$5.55.**

Who has the total value of three dimes and 18 pennies?

I have **$2.02.**

Who has the change you would receive if you paid $5.00 for a magazine that costs $1.95?

I have **$0.48.**

Who has the change you would receive if you paid $11.25 for a book that cost $6.25?

I have **$3.05.**

Who has the total value of one quarter, six dimes, and 15 pennies?

I have **$5.00.**

Who has the total value of six quarters, two dimes, and one nickel?

I have **$1.00.**

Who has the total value of two quarters and 17 pennies?

Money

I have **$0.67.**

Who has the total value of two five-dollar bills, three one-dollar bills, and 17 dimes?

I have **$4.01.**

Who has the total value of one quarter, three dimes, two nickels, and one penny?

I have **$14.70.**

Who has the change you would most likely receive if you gave the clerk a twenty-dollar bill and two dimes to pay for shoes that were on sale for $10.20?

I have **$0.66.**

Who has the total value of three quarters, three dimes, and three pennies?

I have **$10.00.**

Who has the total value of three five-dollar bills, six quarters, and one nickel?

I have **$1.08.**

Who has the total value of one quarter, five dimes, and 16 pennies?

I have **$16.55.**

Who has the total value of nineteen dimes, one nickel, and twelve pennies?

I have **$0.91.**

Who has the total value of seven quarters, two nickels, and seven pennies?

I have **$2.07.**

Who has the change you would receive if you bought a taco for $0.99 with a five-dollar bill?

I have **$1.92.**

Who has the change you would receive if you bought three pairs of socks at $1.25 each and you paid with a five-dollar bill?

I Have, Who Has?: Math • 3–4 © 2006 Creative Teaching Press

Money

I have **$1.25.**

Who has the total value of one five-dollar bill, two one-dollar bills, and nine nickels?

I have **$1.23.**

Who has the change you would receive if you bought $0.65 worth of candy with a dollar bill?

I have **$7.45.**

Who has the total value of six nickels and 17 pennies?

I have **$0.35.**

Who has the total value of two quarters and 18 pennies?

I have **$0.47.**

Who has the total value of eight quarters, eight dimes, and eight pennies?

I have **$0.68.**

Who has the change you would receive if you bought 4 pounds of bananas at $0.75 a pound with a five-dollar bill?

I have **$2.88.**

Who has the change you would receive if you bought three candy bars priced at $0.75 each with a five-dollar bill?

I have **$2.00.**

Who has the change you would receive if you gave the clerk $10.00 to pay for two comic books that cost $4.25 each?

I have **$2.75.**

Who has the total value of twelve dimes and three pennies?

I have **$1.50.**

Who has the first card?

Money

Directions: As your classmates identify the answers, write each number in one of the nine empty wallets below. Start with Wallet 1. Go from left to right and top to bottom. After writing a number in Wallet 9 begin again with Wallet 1.

Wallet 1

Wallet 2

Wallet 3

Wallet 4

Wallet 5

Wallet 6

Wallet 7

Wallet 8

Wallet 9

1. Estimate which wallet has the most money. _____

2. Estimate which wallet has the least money. _____

3. If you wanted to buy a new pair of shoes on sale for $15.99 and you had Wallet 5, how much change would you receive? _____

4. If you wanted to buy a new DVD on sale for $7.50 and you had Wallet 3, how much change would you receive? _____

I Have, Who Has?: Math • 3–4 © 2006 Creative Teaching Press

Time

I have the **first card.**

Who has 15 minutes after 4:15?

I have **2:15.**

Who has 15 minutes after 8:45?

I have **4:30.**

Who has 30 minutes after 6:45?

I have **9:00.**

Who has 45 minutes after 11:30?

I have **7:15.**

Who has 45 minutes after 3:00?

I have **12:15.**

Who has 15 minutes after 11:45?

I have **3:45.**

Who has 30 minutes after 2:45?

I have **12:00.**

Who has 1 hour and 15 minutes after 3:00?

I have **3:15.**

Who has 45 minutes after 1:30?

I have **4:15.**

Who has 2 hours and 30 minutes after 7:00?

Time

I have **9:30.**

Who has 1 hour and 45 minutes after 4:30?

I have **7:00.**

Who has 2 and a half hours before 11:00?

I have **6:15.**

Who has 2 and a half hours after 8:30?

I have **8:30.**

Who has 1 hour and 45 minutes after 11:45?

I have **11:00.**

Who has 45 minutes after 10:45?

I have **1:30.**

Who has 3 hours before 2:15?

I have **11:30.**

Who has 1 hour and 15 minutes after 9:00?

I have **11:15.**

Who has 3 and a half hours before 1:30?

I have **10:15.**

Who has 3 and a half hours after 3:30?

I have **10:00.**

Who has 45 minutes before 2:30?

I Have, Who Has?: Math • 3–4 © 2006 Creative Teaching Press

I have **1:45.**

Who has 45 minutes after 4:30?

I have **11:45.**

Who has an hour and a half past 11:00?

I have **5:15.**

Who has an hour and a half before 8:15?

I have **12:30.**

Who has 45 minutes after 12:30?

I have **6:45.**

Who has 3 hours before 1:45?

I have **1:15.**

Who has 2 and a half hours past noon?

I have **10:45.**

Who has a half hour past 8:45?

I have **2:30.**

Who has 45 minutes before 4:15?

I have **9:15.**

Who has 2 hours and 15 minutes before 2:00?

I have **3:30.**

Who has 45 minutes before 6:30?

I Have, Who Has?: Math • 3–4 © 2006 Creative Teaching Press

Time

I have **5:45**.

Who has 45 minutes after 5:45?

I have **8:00**.

Who has 1 hour and a half before 6:30?

I have **6:30**.

Who has 45 minutes before 8:15?

I have **5:00**.

Who has 1 hour and 45 minutes after 4:15?

I have **7:30**.

Who has 1 hour and 45 minutes after 3:00?

I have **6:00**.

Who has 2 hours and 15 minutes before 10:00?

I have **4:45**.

Who has a half hour before 3:15?

I have **7:45**.

Who has 1 hour and 45 minutes after 6:30?

I have **2:45**.

Who has 1 hour and a half past 6:30?

I have **8:15**.

Who has the first card?

I Have, Who Has?: Math • 3–4 © 2006 Creative Teaching Press

Time

Directions: As your classmates identify the answers, write each time in the grid from left to right and top to bottom.

Blue →										
Red										
Green										
Orange										3:15

Write the times from the blue and green rows under the first two clocks. Calculate the difference between the two times and write your answers under the third clock.

Blue (a.m.)	Green (p.m.)	Difference in Time

_____   _____   _____

_____   _____   _____

_____   _____   _____

_____   _____   _____

_____   _____   _____

_____   _____   _____

_____   _____   _____

_____   _____   _____

_____   _____   _____

Measurement

I have the **first card**.

Who has the area of a square with sides of 4 inches each?

I have **24 cups**.

Who has the number of ounces in 2 pounds?

I have **16 square inches**.

Who has the perimeter of a rectangle that is 4 inches by 5 inches?

I have **32 ounces**.

Who has the number of inches in 1 yard?

I have **18 inches**.

Who has the number of pints in 3 quarts?

I have **36 inches**.

Who has the area of a rectangle with sides measuring 6 inches by 9 inches?

I have **6 pints**.

Who has the number of quarts in 5 gallons?

I have **54 square inches**.

Who has the perimeter of a rectangular tabletop measuring 2 feet by 9 feet?

I have **20 quarts**.

Who has the number of cups in 12 pints?

I have **22 feet**.

Who has the number of gallons equal to 20 quarts?

I Have, Who Has?: Math • 3–4 © 2006 Creative Teaching Press

Measurement

I have **5 gallons**.

Who has the number of eggs in seven dozen?

I have **49 square inches**.

Who has the number of inches in 6 feet?

I have **84 eggs**.

Who has the number of pints in 14 quarts?

I have **72 inches**.

Who has the perimeter of a rectangle measuring 7 inches by 12 inches?

I have **28 pints**.

Who has the number of quarts in 12 gallons?

I have **38 inches**.

Who has the number of hours equal to 240 minutes?

I have **48 quarts**.

Who has the number of yards equal to 36 feet?

I have **4 hours**.

Who has the number of tons equal to 16,000 pounds?

I have **12 yards**.

Who has the area of a square with equal sides measuring 7 inches?

I have **8 tons**.

Who has the number of years equal to 36 months?

Measurement

I have **3 years**.

Who has the number of miles equal to 3,520 yards?

I have **2 miles**.

Who has the perimeter of a parallelogram measuring 5 inches by 2 inches?

I have **14 inches**.

Who has the number of meters in 10 decimeters?

I have **1 meter**.

Who has the number of kilometers in 100,000 meters?

I have **100 kilometers**.

Who has the number of minutes in an hour and a half?

I have **90 minutes**.

Who has the number of quarts equal to 28 cups?

I have **7 quarts**.

Who has the area of a square with sides of 9 inches each?

I have **81 square inches**.

Who has the number of gallons equal to 72 pints?

I have **9 gallons**.

Who has the number of years equal to 132 months?

I have **11 years**.

Who has the number of ounces in 5 pounds?

I Have, Who Has?: Math • 3–4 © 2006 Creative Teaching Press

Measurement

I have **80 ounces**.

Who has the perimeter of a rectangle measuring 8 inches by 15 inches?

I have **88 cups**.

Who has the number of quarts in 15 gallons?

I have **46 inches**.

Who has the number of hours in 600 minutes?

I have **60 quarts**.

Who has the perimeter of a rhombus that measures 10 inches on each side?

I have **10 hours**.

Who has the area of a parallelogram that measures 8 inches on each side?

I have **40 inches**.

Who has the number of cups in 33 pints?

I have **64 square inches**.

Who has the number of inches in 8 feet?

I have **66 cups**.

Who has the area of a square that measures 5 inches on each side?

I have **96 inches**.

Who has the number of cups in 44 pints?

I have **25 square inches**.

Who has the first card?

Measurement

Directions: Complete the maze by highlighting the answers as your classmates identify them.

12 centimeters	**Start** *	6 feet	80 ounces	46 inches	32 feet
15 quarts	16 square inches	9 gallons	11 years	10 hours	64 square inches
6 pints	18 inches	81 square inches	7 quarts	90 minutes	96 inches
20 quarts	24 cups	18 feet	2 inches	100 kilometers	88 cups
36 inches	32 ounces	8 tons	3 years	1 meter	60 quarts
54 square inches	5 inches	4 hours	2 miles	14 inches	40 inches
22 feet	48 eggs	38 inches	72 inches	18 eggs	66 cups
5 gallons	16 centimeters	4 square inches	49 square inches	32 centimeters	**Finish** 25 square inches
84 eggs	28 pints	48 quarts	12 yards	22 square inches	20 centimeters

1. Draw a figure that has a perimeter in centimeters equal to the number in the first box that is **not** highlighted above.

2. Draw a figure that has an area in centimeters equal to the number in the 10th box that is **not** highlighted above.

3. Draw a figure that has a perimeter in centimeters equal to the number in the last box that is **not** highlighted above.

I Have, Who Has?: Math • 3–4 © 2006 Creative Teaching Press

Probability

Note: Make a copy of the Probability Overhead Transparency reproducible (page 186) on an overhead transparency. Display the overhead transparency while students play the game.

I have the **first card.**

Who has the fraction that shows the chance of spinning a "B" on Spinner 4?

I have **3/8.**

Who has the fraction that shows the chance of pulling a black chip out of Bag 3?

I have 2/4 **reduced to 1/2.**

Who has the fraction that shows the chance of pulling a black chip out of Bag 1?

I have **1/8.**

Who has the fraction that shows the chance of **not** spinning blue on Spinner 7?

I have **0.**

Who has the fraction that shows the chance of flipping over a card labeled "M" from Card Set 1?

I have **3/4.**

Who has the fraction that shows the chance of spinning a "3" on Spinner 2?

I have 3/6 **reduced to 1/2.**

Who has the fraction that shows the chance of spinning a "T" on Spinner 5?

I have 2/8 **reduced to 1/4.**

Who has the fraction that shows the chance of spinning red or blue on Spinner 1?

I have **1/4.**

Who has the fraction that shows the chance of spinning a "5" on Spinner 9?

I have **5/8.**

Who has the fraction that shows the chance of pulling a green chip out of Bag 2?

Probability

 I have ⁶⁄₇.

Who has the fraction that shows the chance of flipping over a card labeled "Z" from Card Set 2?

 I have **Bag 2.**

Who has the fraction that shows the chance of flipping over a card labeled "X" if you use Card Set 2?

 I have ⁷⁄₁₂.

Who has the color you have a ⅓ chance of spinning on Spinner 3?

 I have ³⁄₁₂ **reduced to ¼.**

Who has the bag you would most likely choose to use if pulling out a black chip meant you won a free magazine?

 I have **blue.**

Who has the color you will most likely spin if you use Spinner 8?

 I have **Bag 3.**

Who has the fraction that shows the chance of pulling either a yellow or pink chip out of Bag 1?

 I have **red.**

Who has the fraction that shows the chance of flipping over a red card if you use Card Set 3?

 I have ²⁄₁₀ **reduced to ⅕.**

Who has the fraction that shows the chance of flipping over a card labeled "A" using Card Set 1?

 I have ⁴⁄₈ **reduced to ½.**

Who has the bag you would most likely choose to use if pulling out a green chip meant winning $10.00?

 I have ²⁄₆ **reduced to ⅓.**

Who has the fraction that shows the chance of spinning blue if you use Spinner 6?

Probability

I have ⅓.

Who has the spinner you would choose to use if spinning blue won you the first turn in a game—Spinner 1 or Spinner 3?

I have ⅙.

Who has the fraction that shows the chance of flipping over a card labeled "X" or "Y" from Card Set 2?

I have **Spinner 3.**

Who has the fraction that shows the chance of pulling a red chip out of Bag 1?

I have ⁵⁄₁₂.

Who has the fraction that shows the chance of **not** getting a yellow card from Card Set 3?

I have ⁴⁄₁₀ **reduced to** ⅖.

Who has the fraction that shows the chance of spinning either purple or green on Spinner 6?

I have ⅞.

Who has the spinner you would choose to use if spinning blue earned you something that you wanted—Spinner 1 or Spinner 8?

I have ⅔.

Who has the fraction that shows the chance of pulling a blue chip out of Bag 2?

I have **Spinner 1.**

Who has the spinner you would choose to use if spinning green earned you something that you wanted—Spinner 6 or Spinner 8?

I have ⅟₇.

Who has the fraction that shows the chance of flipping over a card labeled "F" from Card Set 1?

I have **Spinner 6.**

Who has the spinner you would choose to use if spinning an odd number meant you won the game—Spinner 2 or Spinner 9?

Probability

I have **Spinner 9.**

Who has the fraction that shows the chance of **not** pulling a blue or an orange chip out of Bag 3?

I have **Spinner 2.**

Who has the bag you would rather use if pulling out a red chip meant winning something you really wanted—Bag 1 or Bag 3?

I have ⁶⁄₈ **reduced to ¾.**

Who has the fraction that shows the chance of flipping over a card labeled "Y" from Card Set 2?

I have **Bag 1.**

Who has the card set you would rather use if flipping over a vowel meant losing all your points in a game—Card Set 1 or Card Set 2?

I have ²⁄₁₂ **reduced to ⅙.**

Who has the fraction that shows the chance of flipping over a card **not** labeled "X" from Card Set 2?

I have **Card Set 2.**

Who has the color you will most likely pull out of Bag 2?

I have ⁹⁄₁₂ **reduced to ¾.**

Who has the fraction that shows the chance of pulling a purple chip out of Bag 1?

I have **green.**

Who has the spinner you would most likely choose to use if spinning blue meant going first in the game— Spinner 7 or Spinner 8?

I have ¹⁄₁₀.

Who has the spinner you would rather use if spinning a number less than 10 wins you the first turn in a game—Spinner 9 or Spinner 2?

I have **Spinner 7.**

Who has the first card?

I Have, Who Has?: Math • 3–4 © 2006 Creative Teaching Press

Probability

Directions: Complete the maze by highlighting the answers as your classmates identify them.

Why do fish live in salt water?

¹⁄₇ Z	¹⁄₆ A	⁵⁄₁₂ F	⁷⁄₈ H	Spinner 1 I	²⁄₃ O	Bag 3 G
²⁄₃ S	¹⁄₃ M	²⁄₆ or ¹⁄₃ E	³⁄₅ B	Spinner 6 C	³⁄₅ E	**Finish** Spinner 7
⁴⁄₁₀ or ²⁄₅ K	Spinner 3 M	²⁄₁₀ or ¹⁄₅ E	⁵⁄₇ C	Spinner 9 C	²⁄₇ A	green D
Bag 1 U	³⁄₄ S	Bag 3 S	⁴⁄₉ E	⁶⁄₈ or ³⁄₄ R	¹⁄₉ P	Card Set 2 I
⁵⁄₇ E	²⁄₅ P	³⁄₁₂ or ¹⁄₄ T	Bag 4 P	²⁄₁₂ or ¹⁄₆ B	Spinner 2 Y	Bag 1 Z
red O	⁴⁄₈ or ¹⁄₂ A	Bag 2 B	³⁄₄ E	⁹⁄₁₂ or ³⁄₄ S	¹⁄₁₀ R	⁵⁄₆ R
blue T	purple M	Spinner 5 A	¹⁄₄ K	³⁄₈ E	Spinner 4 S	²⁄₃ T
⁷⁄₁₂ Z	⁶⁄₇ O	⁵⁄₈ F	²⁄₈ or ¹⁄₄ F	³⁄₄ N	¹⁄₈ D	³⁄₈ I
Spinner 2 H	¹⁄₅ E	Bag 1 M	³⁄₅ S	Bag 7 N	⁴⁄₉ E	¹⁄₄ I
Bag 2 E	³⁄₈ Z	Spinner 7 E	**Start** *	²⁄₄ or ¹⁄₂ R	0 S	³⁄₆ or N

Cross out the first two boxes that are **not** highlighted above. Write the letters that are **not** highlighted or c
on the blanks below to reveal the answer to the riddle. Write the letters in order from left to right and to

___ ___ ___ ___ ___ ___ ___ ___ ___   ___ ___ ___ ___ ___ ___

___ ___ ___ ___ ___ ___ ___ ___ ___   ___ ___ ___ ___ ___

Draw a spinner that shows a ³⁄₅ chance of spinning red.

I have **30.**

Who has the number of ways the baker can make an ice-cream cake if she has six ice-cream flavors, four cake mixes, and three frosting flavors to choose from?

I have **28.**

Who has the number of different ways the sweet treats can be combined into gift baskets if there are six types of cookies, two types of brownies, and five types of fudge?

I have **72.**

Who has the number of different ways the cheerleader can dress if she has three skirts, four tops, and two pairs of socks?

I have **60.**

Who has the number of different ways of arranging the aquarium if the store sells three types of rocks, two types of aquariums, and three types of fish?

I have **24.**

o has the number of ways the candy er can package the extra candies if are ten chocolates, three caramels, and three sour strip flavors?

I have **18.**

Who has the number of different ways of decorating the table for a party if there are seven different tablecloths, three types of dishes, and one centerpiece?

I have **90.**

n as the number of ways the an be made if there are five ortilla chips, three types of and three types of salsa?

I have **21.**

Who has the number of different ways a homemade card can be created if there are two types of paper, four types of decorations, and four types of bows?

I have **45.**

Who ha e number of ways the bracelets n be made if there are four types wire, seven types of beads, an one type of clasp?

I have **32.**

Who has the number of different ways a hamburger can be made if there are two types of buns, one type of meat, and four types of toppings?

I Have, Who Has?: Math • 3–4 © 2006 Creative Teaching Press

All Possible Outcomes

I have **8.**

Who has the number of different ways a letter can be mailed if there are five types of envelopes, eight types of stamps, and two types of address labels?

I have **20.**

Who has the number of different ways that an ice-cream sundae can be made if you have six types of ice cream, one type of chocolate syrup, and eleven different toppings?

I have **80.**

Who has the number of different ways a baby can be dressed if there are two types of diapers, ten T-shirts, and two pairs of shorts?

I have **66.**

Who has the number of different ways that a salad can be made if you have three types of croutons, three dressings, and nine types of lettuce to choose from?

I have **40.**

Who has the number of different ways that birthday grab bags can be created if there are five types of horns, five types of hats, and two types of funny glasses?

I have **81.**

Who has the number of different ways a room can be redecorated if there are two types of wallpaper and five paint colors to choose from?

I have **50.**

Who has the number of different ways that marshmallow cereal bars can be made for a classroom party if there are three types of cereal, two types of marshmallows, and nine types of candies?

I have **10.**

Who has the number of different ways a sandwich can be made at the local sandwich shop if it offers three types of bread, three types of meat, and seven toppings?

I have **54.**

Who has the number of different ways that a taco can be made if there are two types of shells, two types of meat, and five types of cheese?

I have **63.**

Who has the number of different ways a pool can be built if there are two types of plaster, two types of paint, and eleven types of rock?

I have **44.**

Who has the number of different ways a clown can decorate her face if she has five types of noses and five face paint colors?

I have 77.

Who has the number of different ways that the card you created on the Internet can be printed if there are two ink colors, six types of paper, and seven animals to choose from?

I have **25.**

Who has the number of different ways a puppy can be dressed up if there are two types of hats, four types of jackets, and eight T-shirts?

I have **84.**

Who has the number of different ways that the kid's meal can be ordered from the fast food restaurant if there are two types of fries, four types of chicken, and eleven different toys?

I have **64.**

Who has the number of different ways a pie can be baked if there are three types of shells and three types of fruit in the refrigerator?

I have **88.**

Who has the number of different ways that the gourmet pretzel can be ordered if there are two different sizes and seven different toppings?

I have **9.**

Who has the number of different ways that a fruit salad can be made if there are seven types of citrus fruit, four types of berries, and two types of melon?

I have **14.**

Who has the number of different ways that a soccer player can get ready for a game if he has seven different pairs of socks and five jerseys?

I have **56.**

Who has the number of different ways that the teacher can create goodie bags if she has seven types of bookmarks and eleven types of carnival toys?

I have **35.**

Who has the first card?

I Have, Who Has?: Math • 3–4 © 2006 Creative Teaching Press

All Possible Outcomes

Directions: Highlight the answers as your classmates identify them.

1	2	3	4	5	6	7	8	9	10
11	12	13	14	15	16	17	18	19	20
21	22	23	24	25	26	27	28	29	30
31	32	33	34	35	36	37	38	39	40
41	42	43	44	45	46	47	48	49	50
51	52	53	54	55	56	57	58	59	60
61	62	63	64	65	66	67	68	69	70
71	72	73	74	75	76	77	78	79	80
81	82	83	84	85	86	87	88	89	90
91	92	93	94	95	96	97	98	99	100

Choose one number that is highlighted in the table above. Create a story like the ones in the game. Draw a diagram to represent that many outcomes in the space below.

Data Analysis

Note: Make a copy of the Data Analysis Overhead Transparency reproducible (page 197) on an overhead transparency. Display the overhead transparency while students play the game.

I have the **first card.**

Who has the type of graph shown in Data Set 4?

I have **ice-cream sundaes.**

Who has the least popular type of book read over the summer in Data Set 4?

I have a **bar graph.**

Who has the number of cans collected by Mr. Olson's class in one month?

I have **biography.**

Who has two types of desserts chosen by exactly 15 people in Room 26?

I have **438.**

Who has the lowest temperature in June recorded in Data Set 5?

I have **cookies and brownies.**

Who has the highest temperature in June according to Data Set 5?

I have **about 52 degrees.**

Who has the type of chart shown in Data Set 1?

I have **about 89 degrees.**

Who has the name of the chart shown in Data Sets 2 and 3?

I have a **tally chart.**

Who has the most popular dessert as shown in Data Set 3?

I have **organized tables.**

Who has the type of book that was chosen 15 times over the summer?

I Have, Who Has?: Math • 3–4 © 2006 Creative Teaching Press

Data Analysis

I have **adventure.**

Who has the number of people who were in Room 26 on the day the graph was made?

I have a **line graph.**

Who has the data set that shows change over time?

I have **34.**

Who has the classroom teacher whose students collected the most cans by Week 2?

I have **Data Set 5.**

Who has the total number of cans collected the first week?

I have **Mrs. Guzman.**

Who has the number of fantasy and mystery books that were read?

I have **312.**

Who has the two types of books exactly 20 students read?

I have **30.**

Who has the two desserts chosen as favorites by exactly 20 people?

I have **biographies and adventures.**

Who has the total number of students who did not choose pie or cookies as their favorite dessert?

I have **ice-cream sundaes and cookies.**

Who has the type of graph shown in Data Set 5?

I have **24.**

Who has the difference between the highest and lowest temperatures on the first fifteen days of June?

I have about **37 degrees.**

Who has the two hottest days of June as shown in the line graph?

I have **June 5th and 8th.**

Who has the coldest day of June as shown in the line graph?

I have **June 3rd.**

Who has the total number of books read over the summer?

I have **75.**

Who has the room that read the most books as recorded in the tally chart?

I have **Room 11.**

Who has the week in which the classrooms collected the fewest number of cans according to Data Set 2?

I have **Week 3.**

Who has the difference in the number of books read by the students in Room 12 and those read by Room 15?

I have **7.**

Who has the average (mean) number of books read per student if there are 20 students in Room 11?

I have **2.**

Who has the difference in temperatures on the first and fifteenth days of June?

I have about **18 degrees.**

Who has the difference between the number of mysteries read and the total number of adventures and nature books read?

I have **20.**

Who has the desserts that were equally popular?

Data Analysis

I have **pie and fruit.**

Who has the total number of books read in all rooms, according to the tally chart?

I have **Week 4.**

Who has the number of books read in Room 13 that were more than those read in Room 12?

I have **146.**

Who has the difference between the number of cans collected by Mr. Olsen's class and Mr. Nguyen's class in Week 1?

I have **9.**

Who has the difference between the best and worst week Mrs. Guzman's class had in collecting cans?

I have **43.**

Who has the two types of books that were read over the summer that equaled exactly 40 books?

I have **137.**

Who has the difference in votes between the most and least popular dessert choices?

I have the **adventure and nature books.**

Who has the number of books read by rooms 11 and 14?

I have **10.**

Who has the total number of cans collected by Mr. Nguyen's class?

I have **75.**

Who has the week in which the most cans were collected for the food drive?

I have **371.**

Who has the first card?

Data Analysis

Directions: Complete the maze by highlighting the answers as your classmates identify them.

Start *	bar graph	line graph	nature
organized table	438	organized tables	adventure
tally chart	about 52 degrees	about 89 degrees	34
ice-cream sundaes	biography	cookies and brownies	Mrs. Guzman
about 37 degrees	24	brownies and pie	30
June 5th and 8th	biographies and adventures	line graph	ice-cream sundaes and cookies
June 3rd	312	Data Set 5	Data Set 2
75	222	Data Set 3	300
Room 11	Room 12	9	137
Week 3	50 degrees	Week 4	10
7	52	75	**Finish** 371
2	12	adventure and nature books	200
about 18 degrees	biographies and nature books	43	nature books
20	pie and fruit	146	150

Think of a question (e.g., What is your favorite color?) to ask 10 classmates. Create a bar graph that shows the data you collected on the back of this paper.

Write three things you notice about your graph.

1. _____

2. _____

3. _____

I Have, Who Has?: Math • 3–4 © 2006 Creative Teaching Press

Data Analysis Overhead Transparency

Data Set 1

Number of Books Read Per Class

Room 11	卌 卌 卌 卌 卌 卌 卌 卌
Room 12	卌 卌 卌 卌 III
Room 13	卌 卌 卌 卌 卌 卌 II
Room 14	卌 卌 卌 卌 卌 卌 卌
Room 15	卌 卌 卌 I

Data Set 2

Cans Collected by Fourth Grade Classes in One Month

	Week 1	Week 2	Week 3	Week 4
Mr. Olson	124	96	55	163
Mr. Nguyen	81	99	62	129
Mrs. Guzman	107	142	44	181

Data Set 3

Favorite Desserts in Room 26

Dessert	Total Number of Votes
cookies	7
brownies	8
ice cream sundaes	13
fruit	3
pie	3

Data Set 4

Kinds of Books Read During Summer

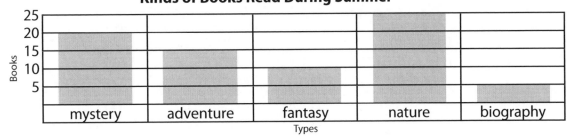

Data Set 5

Daily Temperatures in the First Half of June

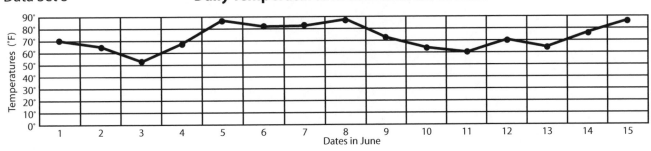

Answer Key

Number Sense (Page 10)

Start →	14	77	54	48	96	81	26	61	45
59	52	78	89	28	25	69	46	73	64
39	34	43	23	67	85	66	56	42	92
41	38	83	63	65	74	75	49	68	87
A	B	C	D	E	F	G	H	I	J

1. 51 2. 85 3. 51
4. 35 5. 74 6. 66
7. 36 8. 52 9. 86
10. 63 11. 64 12. 37

Number Sense—Making 100 (Page 15)

1	2	3	4	5	6	7	8	9	10
11	12	13	14	15	16	17	18	19	20
21	22	23	24	25	26	27	28	29	30
31	32	33	34	35	36	37	38	39	40
41	42	43	44	45	46	47	48	49	50
51	52	53	54	55	56	57	58	59	60
61	62	63	64	65	66	67	68	69	70
71	72	73	74	75	76	77	78	79	80
81	82	83	84	85	86	87	88	89	90
91	92	93	94	95	96	97	98	99	100

Answers will vary.

Subtraction—Dropping Common Zeros (Page 20)

Start *	330	360	250	240	350	160
30	280	430	470	140	170	150
70	380	260	220	10	20	130
600	180	290	120	80	190	50
700	400	560	310	300	270	390
110	200	90	100	500	460	440
60	550	210	340	380	370	350
50	40	230	480	320	280	Finish 330

Answers will vary.

Adding from Left to Right (Page 25)

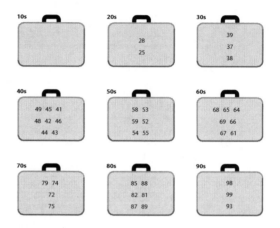

Answers will vary.

Place Value 1 (Page 30)

6 ones or 6	2 tens or 20	7 tens or 70	Start	8 tens or 80	1 hundred or 100	5 tens or 50
3 hundreds or 300	4 ones or 4	6 hundred	8 thousands or 8,000	3 tens or 30	5 thousands or 5,000	8 hundreds or 800
1 thousand or 1,000	5 ones or 5	9 hundred	2 tens or 20	9 ones or 9	6 ones or 6	2 thousands or 2,000
0 tens or 0	7 thousands or 7,000	3 thousand	0 tens or 0	4 ones or 4	0 tens or 0	6 hundreds or 600
2 tens or 20	8 ones or 8	1 hundred or 100	4 tens or 40	3 ones or 3	2 hundreds or 200	9 hundreds or 900
8 hundred	5 hundred	1 thousand	2 ones or 2	4 thousands or 4,000	6 tens or 60	3 thousands or 3,000
7 tens or 70	3 ones or 3	1 one or 1	6 ones or 6	9 tens or 90	9 thousands or 9,000	4 hundreds or 400
8 tens or 80	0 ones or 0	1 ten or 10	6 thousands or 6,000	5 tens or 50	3 ones or 3	8 tens or 80
5 tens or 50	Finish ones place	9 ones or 9	7 ones or 7	5 hundreds or 500	8 thousands or 8,000	7 hundreds or 700

Answers for 1–3 will vary.

Place Value 2 (Page 35)

1 hundred thousand or 100,000	834,600	80,346	56,889	2 ten thousands or 20,000	8 hundred thousands or 800,000	4 ten thousands or 40,000
60,542	409,329	5 ten thousands or 50,000	47,602	9 hundred thousands or 900,000	582,110	Start
654,200	4 hundred thousands or 400,000	925,360	6 ten thousands or 60,000	534,299	48,992	774,294
555,555	832,007	3 hundred thousands or 300,000	407,602	5 thousands or 5,000	92,360	201,101
1 ten thousand or 10,000	8 ten thousands or 80,000	83,027	7 hundred thousands or 700,000	198,002	5 hundred thousands or 500,000	750,200
250,402	24,550	981,203	39,702	6 hundred thousands or 600,000	846,294	3 ten thousands or 30,000
Finish 74,365	444,301	402,309	9 ten thousands or 90,000	10,982	384,927	75,200
430,998	20,909	723,948	354,000	7 ten thousands or 70,000	3,509	2 hundred thousands or 200,000

Answers for 1–4 will vary.

Making Sets of Ten (Page 40)

1 R	2 B	3 T	4 E	5 H	6 C	7 Y	8 C	9 A	10 A
11 N	12 O	13 T	14 S	15 I	16 U	17 S	18 S	19 K	20 L
21 O	22 E	23 M	24 C	25 R	26 T	27 U	28 H	29 P	30 E
31 S	32 E	33 T	34 R	35 M	36 Y	37 A	38 W	39 B	40 J
41 O	42 K	43 A	44 E	45 N	46 E	47 S	48 P	49 O	50 M
51 S	52 P	53 H	54 A	55 I	56 T	57 L	58 C	59 O	60 H
61 H	62 E	63 I	64 U	65 S	66 H	67 A	68 E	69 L	70 I
71 O	72 R	73 V	74 E	75 E	76 Y	77 R	78 E	79 Y	80 S
81 O	82 S	83 U	84 L	85 N	86 P	87 T	88 E	89 V	90 M
91 I	92 E	93 L	94 L	95 L	96 E	97 E	98 D	99 A	100 I

Because they keep their eyes peeled

Multiplication 1 (Page 45)

Start →	10	40	4	25	60	20	7	6	35
3	30	8	90	12	15	14	45	2	50
16	9	5	0	36	70	24	18	80	28
32	1	100	11	21	31	26	99	51	49
A	B	C	D	E	F	G	H	I	J

Equations will vary.
Column E = 94

Multiplication 2 (Page 50)

Start →	25	12	18	30	9	8	6	15	70
20	24	36	10	16	35	42	5	21	32
4	40	50	3	27	48	28	45	60	54
80	90	100	13	19	26	22	37	31	41
A	B	C	D	E	F	G	H	I	J

Equations will vary.
Column G = 100

Multiplication 3 (Page 55)

64	18	12	55	40	70	6	7	60	4	59
42	36	30	20	28	8	25	50	40	81	41
Start	12	9	33	27	14	36	72	56	42	33
35	16	21	32	63	48	54	21	10	50	Finish 65
15	20	24	8	16	35	45	80	49	64	36

Equations will vary.

Multiplication 4 (Page 60)

1 L	2 M	3 T	4 O	5 H	6 C	7 O	8 C	9 A	10 M
11 E	12 N	13 I	14 S	15 I	16 U	17 G	18 S	19 K	20 A
21 U	22 E	23 T	24 C	25 R	26 T	27 U	28 H	29 P	30 W
31 P	32 T	33 T	34 R	35 M	36 Y	37 I	38 W	39 B	40 H
41 R	42 K	43 M	44 E	45 S	46 E	47 E	48 P	49 O	50 X
51 B	52 P	53 N	54 A	55 E	56 T	57 O	58 C	59 O	60 L
61 L	62 E	63 U	64 E	65 H	66 S	67 E	68 E	69 L	70 I
71 M	72 R	73 V	74 E	75 R	76 Y	77 R	78 E	79 Y	80 H
81 S	82 S	83 E	84 L	85 L	86 P	87 A	88 E	89 V	90 S

"Long time no sea!"

Working with Doubles (Page 65)

Red →	36	81	16	25	49	100	4	64	9	1
Blue	15	65	39	19	5	71	90	37	6	74
Pink	10	48	82	24	14	11	99	46	17	3
Green	91	110	63	101	2	80	59	54	50	100

$6 \times 6 = 36$

$9 \times 9 = 81$

$4 \times 4 = 16$

$5 \times 5 = 25$

$7 \times 7 = 49$

$10 \times 10 = 100$

$2 \times 2 = 4$

$8 \times 8 = 64$

$3 \times 3 = 9$

$1 \times 1 = 1$

Addition, Subtraction, and Multiplication (Page 70)

50	19	38	10	27	44	83	89	86	99	Finish 100	28
69	36	90	40	5	21	47	64	90	82	12	36
48	54	72	34	42	53	70	31	52	46	39	15
77	55	80	16	30	88	54	18	26	22	30	28
62	33	35	Start	45	24	63	20	41	57	65	49

Equations will vary.

Division 1 (Page 75)

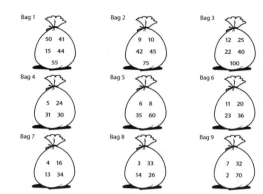

1. 90

2. 30

3. 67

4. 1

5. 90

6. 9

Division 2 (Page 80)

1 S	2 A	3 M	4 I	5 R	6 O	7 O	8 W	9 N	10 R
11 M	12 L	13 N	14 I	15 I	16 N	17 G	18 D	19 K	20 A
21 A	22 E	23 T	24 C	25 R	26 T	27 U	28 Y	29 P	30 N
31 R	32 E	33 T	34 R	35 M	36 O	37 I	38 U	39 B	40 H
41 O	42 K	43 M	44 E	45 S	46 L	47 E	48 O	49 O	50 O
51 O	52 P	53 N	54 O	55 E	56 K	57 O	58 A	59 O	60 L
61 P	62 L	63 I	64 I	65 E	66 H	67 S	68 T	69 L	70 I
71 B	72 T	73 L	74 L	75 R	76 E	77 R	78 F	79 Y	80 H
81 A	82 L	83 E	84 U	85 L	86 S	87 A	88 E	89 V	90 S
91 O	92 H	93 I	94 E	95 T	96 D	97 A	98 H	99 N	100 S

"You look a little flushed!"

Basic Operations (Page 85)

Boat →	34	16	53	68	6	80	38	60	58	54
Canoe	91	28	26	15	24	49	81	83	9	45
Ship	32	35	82	21	40	27	46	36	52	50
Yacht	59	5	3	20	4	12	29	100	44	1

Equations will vary.

Balanced Equations 1 (Page 90)

START 3 × 4	75 × 2
6 × 12	49 ÷ 7
4 × 5	88 ÷ 8
3 × 6	75 × 2
6 × 12	100 ÷ 10
6 × 8	49 ÷ 7
84 ÷ 2	15 × 4
12 × 8	3 × 4
5 × 5	49 ÷ 7
5 × 5 + 2	3 × 11
11 × 2	25 × 2
4 × 5	5 × 7
100 ÷ 10	9 × 5
21 × 4	3 × 6
25 × 2	3 × 3 × 11
75 × 2	2 × 2 × 2
6 × 12	49 ÷ 7
4 × 4	84 ÷ 2
36 ÷ 6	6 × 12

6 × 6	3 × 3 × 3 × 2
8 × 11 − 7	2 × 2 × 10
3 × 6	75 × 2
25 ÷ 5	100 ÷ 10
6 × 5 − 1	9 × 7
100 ÷ 10	84 ÷ 2
64 ÷ 2	5 × 5
3 × 4	6 × 4
6 × 12	6 × 5
6 × 5 − 1	4 × 5
2 × 2 × 2	30 ÷ 2
100 ÷ 2 − 1	36 ÷ 6
3 × 3 × 11	25 × 2
3 × 7	5 × 5 + 2
8 × 11 − 7	5 × 5
2 × 2 × 2 × 7	3 × 4
49 ÷ 7	11 × 5
2 × 2 × 2	3 × 3 × 3 × 2
5 × 5 + 2	36 ÷ 6
FINISH 100 ÷ 10	6 × 5 − 2

Equations will vary.

Balanced Equations 2 (Page 95)

2 × 3	40 ÷ 20	6 × 4 − 1	3 × 10 + 2 **Finish**
5 × 10 − 2	3 × 3 + 1	77 ÷ 7	7 × 5 − 4
50 ÷ 2 + 1	8 × 4 + 1	6 × 11 − 3	6 × 9 + 1
144 ÷ 12	5 × 11 + 4	3 × 10 + 2	100 ÷ 5
6 × 3	96 ÷ 12	2 × 2 × 2 − 1	8 × 5 − 3
6 × 7 + 1	12 × 2	3 × 3	25 × 2 − 9
75 ÷ 25	12 × 5 + 4	100 ÷ 20	4 × 5 + 2
32 ÷ 8	7 × 11 − 2	2 × 3	5 × 10 + 3
30 ÷ 2	5 × 10 + 3	6 × 9 + 1	12 × 2
7 × 5 − 1	5 × 9 − 1	3 × 3 + 1	77 ÷ 7
5 × 5	4 × 3 + 1	30 ÷ 2	3 × 10 − 2
5 × 11 + 4	5 × 10 − 1	7 × 5 − 4	4 × 5 + 1
7 × 5 − 4	3 × 10 + 2	6 × 3	144 ÷ 12
5 × 4 − 3	144 ÷ 12 + 2	32 ÷ 8	40 ÷ 20
Start *	2 × 3	75 ÷ 25	2 × 3

Equations will vary.

Comparing Fractions (Page 100)

$\frac{3}{8}$	$\frac{5}{12}$	$\frac{1}{6}$	$\frac{3}{20}$	$\frac{4}{9}$	$\frac{3}{4}$	$\frac{3}{7}$	$\frac{17}{20}$	$\frac{2}{9}$
$\frac{7}{10}$	$\frac{1}{7}$	$\frac{1}{2}$	$\frac{5}{8}$	$\frac{2}{5}$	$\frac{1}{20}$	$\frac{9}{10}$	$\frac{3}{11}$	$\frac{5}{9}$
$\frac{1}{15}$	$\frac{4}{5}$	$\frac{6}{7}$	$\frac{3}{10}$	$\frac{7}{12}$	$\frac{1}{4}$	$\frac{2}{6}$	$\frac{1}{8}$	$\frac{4}{7}$
$\frac{9}{11}$	$\frac{2}{15}$	$\frac{4}{11}$	$\frac{5}{6}$	$\frac{2}{3}$	$\frac{1}{5}$	$\frac{1}{3}$	$\frac{1}{9}$	$\frac{7}{8}$
$\frac{5}{7}$	$\frac{1}{10}$	$\frac{1}{12}$	$\frac{7}{9}$	$\frac{8}{9}$	$\frac{2}{7}$	$\frac{7}{15}$	$\frac{3}{5}$	$\frac{11}{12}$

Fractions will vary.

Addition and Subtraction—Fractions (Page 105)

START numerator	denominator
sum	difference
denominator	numerator
sum	difference
$\frac{2}{9}$	$\frac{4}{9}$
$\frac{4}{11}$	$\frac{6}{11}$
$\frac{1}{8}$	$\frac{3}{8}$
$\frac{13}{25}$	$\frac{11}{25}$
$\frac{1}{6}$	$\frac{5}{6}$
$\frac{3}{4}$	$\frac{1}{4}$
$\frac{3}{10}$	$\frac{7}{10}$
$\frac{5}{9}$	$\frac{7}{9}$
$\frac{3}{5}$	$\frac{4}{5}$
$\frac{2}{3}$	$\frac{1}{3}$
$\frac{1}{7}$	$\frac{4}{7}$
$\frac{1}{5}$	$\frac{2}{5}$
$\frac{5}{7}$	$\frac{2}{7}$
$\frac{7}{10}$	$\frac{3}{10}$
$\frac{1}{7}$	$\frac{3}{7}$
$\frac{3}{5}$	$\frac{2}{5}$

$\frac{8}{9}$	$\frac{2}{9}$
$\frac{5}{8}$	$\frac{3}{8}$
$\frac{7}{9}$	$\frac{1}{9}$
$\frac{3}{11}$	$\frac{9}{11}$
$\frac{1}{4}$	$\frac{2}{4}$ or $\frac{1}{2}$
$\frac{2}{7}$	$\frac{5}{7}$
$\frac{1}{6}$	$\frac{5}{6}$
$\frac{7}{15}$	$\frac{11}{15}$
$\frac{4}{5}$	$\frac{3}{5}$
$\frac{7}{8}$	$\frac{2}{8}$
$\frac{3}{4}$	$\frac{1}{4}$
$\frac{2}{3}$	$\frac{1}{3}$
$\frac{5}{11}$	$\frac{7}{11}$
$\frac{5}{12}$	$\frac{11}{12}$
$\frac{2}{9}$	$\frac{4}{9}$
$\frac{3}{8}$	$\frac{1}{8}$
$\frac{5}{12}$	$\frac{7}{12}$
$\frac{9}{10}$	$\frac{3}{10}$
$\frac{4}{7}$	$\frac{3}{7}$
FINISH Good	Thinking!

Answers will vary.

Addition and Subtraction—Mixed Numbers (Page 110)

$6\frac{2}{5}$	$1\frac{1}{10}$	$2\frac{3}{4}$	$6\frac{2}{4}$ or $6\frac{1}{2}$	$2\frac{1}{4}$	$1\frac{1}{3}$	$4\frac{3}{5}$	$4\frac{7}{7}$ or 5	$2\frac{1}{2}$	$6\frac{2}{3}$
$5\frac{2}{5}$	$4\frac{1}{7}$	$5\frac{3}{4}$	$4\frac{5}{8}$	$2\frac{1}{6}$	$6\frac{1}{5}$	$1\frac{3}{6}$ or $1\frac{1}{2}$	$1\frac{4}{4}$ or 2	$7\frac{4}{5}$	$4\frac{4}{5}$
Finish $6\frac{1}{3}$	$5\frac{3}{5}$	$2\frac{4}{5}$	$4\frac{2}{4}$ or $4\frac{1}{2}$	$3\frac{1}{3}$	$4\frac{1}{5}$	$2\frac{3}{6}$ or $2\frac{1}{2}$	$2\frac{1}{3}$	$1\frac{2}{5}$	$7\frac{1}{2}$
$3\frac{4}{6}$	$1\frac{2}{3}$	9	$5\frac{2}{3}$	5	$1\frac{2}{3}$	$7\frac{1}{6}$	8	$2\frac{5}{7}$	$3\frac{1}{5}$
$3\frac{5}{6}$	$6\frac{7}{8}$	$2\frac{4}{4}$ or 3	$\frac{3}{3}$ or 1	$4\frac{3}{8}$	$3\frac{2}{4}$ or $3\frac{1}{2}$	$5\frac{3}{6}$ or $5\frac{1}{2}$	$4\frac{1}{3}$	$3\frac{2}{5}$	$8\frac{1}{3}$
Start *	$3\frac{2}{3}$	$1\frac{5}{6}$	$3\frac{5}{5}$ or 4	$4\frac{2}{3}$	$5\frac{4}{5}$	6	$3\frac{1}{5}$	$3\frac{1}{3}$	7

Answers for 1–5 will vary.

Changing Mixed Numbers to Decimals (Page 115)

Yellow →	4.5	2.33	6.3	5.25	2.3	1.7	3.5	5.1	3.45	6.89
Purple	4.55	1.17	5.3	1.6	3.66	5.29	4.7	3.1	6.9	2.2
Blue	1.47	4.15	6.37	1.3	4.1	2.99	5.13	6.7	2.7	5.9
Green	3.27	6.71	3.9	1.88	4.99	6.2	1.5	2.53	3.7	8.8

Answers for 1–10 will vary.

Changing Decimals to Mixed Numbers (Page 120)

$1\frac{9}{10}$ S	$3\frac{3}{10}$ Y	$4\frac{1}{100}$ U	$2\frac{48}{100}$ E	$2\frac{48}{100}$ S	$6\frac{25}{100}$ R	$1\frac{9}{10}$ O
$6\frac{36}{100}$ P	$3\frac{33}{100}$ H	$6\frac{5}{10}$ A	$5\frac{12}{100}$ P	$6\frac{9}{10}$ N	$6\frac{9}{100}$ U	$5\frac{19}{100}$ A
$2\frac{3}{100}$ C	$7\frac{45}{100}$ T	$4\frac{8}{10}$ I	$3\frac{88}{100}$ M	$4\frac{2}{10}$ A	$1\frac{25}{100}$ W	$2\frac{6}{10}$ M
$2\frac{4}{10}$ S	$2\frac{2}{100}$ I	$1\frac{9}{100}$ L	$2\frac{7}{10}$ L	$1\frac{9}{10}$ T	$5\frac{3}{10}$ I	$5\frac{3}{100}$ O
Finish $3\frac{7}{100}$	$4\frac{17}{100}$ B	$6\frac{6}{100}$ A	$6\frac{81}{100}$ W	$6\frac{8}{10}$ N	$4\frac{44}{100}$ E	$4\frac{4}{10}$ M
$8\frac{2}{100}$ Y	$1\frac{4}{10}$ E	$2\frac{36}{100}$ D	$1\frac{3}{10}$ S	$3\frac{1}{100}$ B	$3\frac{1}{10}$ O	$1\frac{25}{100}$ I
$1\frac{25}{100}$ L	$5\frac{4}{10}$ S	$6\frac{4}{10}$ A	$3\frac{26}{100}$ O	$5\frac{25}{100}$ G	$2\frac{99}{100}$ Y	$1\frac{9}{10}$ L
$2\frac{48}{100}$ R	$1\frac{87}{100}$ T	$4\frac{9}{10}$ Y	$1\frac{72}{100}$ H	$3\frac{7}{10}$ I	$1\frac{2}{10}$ O	**Start** *

"Put it on my bill."
Answers will vary.

Comparing Decimals (Page 125)

1.9	2.34	4.3	2.05	2.75	5.05	3.13	4.25	1.5	2.25
3.7	1.07	4.7	4.19	3.34	5.25	3.54	6.7	5.8	2.45
4.8	3.67	5.4	4.5	5.7	3.24	4.4	2.06	3.4	5.09
4.65	2.56	1.32	5.06	5.9	3.9	2.98	.75	5.5	4.4
A	B	C	D	E	F	G	H	I	J

A. 1.9 < 3.7 < 4.65 < 4.8
B. 1.07 < 2.34 < 2.56 < 3.67
C. 1.32 < 4.3 < 4.7 < 5.4
D. 2.05 < 4.19 < 4.5 < 5.06
E. 2.75 < 3.34 < 5.7 < 5.9
F. 3.24 < 3.9 < 5.05 < 5.25
G. 2.98 < 3.13 < 3.54 < 4.4
H. 0.75 < 2.06 < 4.25 < 6.7
I. 1.5 < 3.4 < 5.5 < 5.8
J. 2.25 < 2.45 < 4.4 < 5.09

Comparing Mixed Numbers and Decimals (Page 130)

$5\frac{3}{10}$	T	$5\frac{9}{10}$	H	$1\frac{5}{6}$	E	3.67	E	$1\frac{1}{10}$	P
5.49	Y	3.5	M	$2\frac{7}{8}$	A	2.23	F	$2\frac{8}{9}$	A
2.35	B	$5\frac{4}{5}$	U	4.04	M	1.9	Q	$5\frac{1}{10}$	I
$3\frac{4}{5}$	N	$1\frac{1}{10}$	K	4.88	E	4.37	A	3.8	W
Start *		$1\frac{5}{6}$	B	1.45	O	$5\frac{9}{10}$	C	3.37	D
$5\frac{9}{10}$	O	$3\frac{7}{10}$	S	5.89	S	$4\frac{4}{5}$	T	5.49	A
4.88	S	$5\frac{1}{6}$	B	5.15	E	$3\frac{3}{5}$	L	$4\frac{3}{8}$	R
$3\frac{7}{9}$	C	3.67	B	2.28	U	2.35	O	3.97	F
5.5	M	$3\frac{1}{3}$	O	1.45	T	$4\frac{4}{10}$	S	$5\frac{3}{10}$	D
Finish	5.81	$2\frac{2}{3}$	P	3.67	O	$5\frac{1}{3}$	R	3.5	Y
$5\frac{3}{10}$	S	$1\frac{5}{6}$	Y	$4\frac{3}{10}$	A	5.299	H	$2\frac{7}{8}$	H

They make boo-boos.
Answers for 1–4 will vary.

Number Patterns—Addition and Multiplication (Page 135)

1	2	3	4	5	6	7	8	9	10
11	12	13	14	15	16	17	18	19	20
21	22	23	24	25	26	27	28	29	30
31	32	33	34	35	36	37	38	39	40
41	42	43	44	45	46	47	48	49	50
51	52	53	54	55	56	57	58	59	60
61	62	63	64	65	66	67	68	69	70
71	72	73	74	75	76	77	78	79	80
81	82	83	84	85	86	87	88	89	90
91	92	93	94	95	96	97	98	99	100
101	102	103	104	105	106	107	108	109	110
111	112	113	114	115	116	117	118	119	120
A	B	C	D	E	F	G	H	I	J

Answers for 1–8 will vary.

Number Patterns—Subtraction and Division (Page 140)

20	92	47	10	19	12	11	55	72	25
15	7	18	41	23	24	2	33	8	5
21	34	13	36	50	29	28	45	4	6
3	99	9	16	22	60	89	63	68	22
A	B	C	D	E	F	G	H	I	J

Answers for 1–12 will vary.

Number Patterns—All Operations (Page 145)

Start*	60	A	44	L	22	K	31	S	20	S	56	P	22	M	16	T	30	V
45	C	14	T	100	O	40	D	45	P	35	G	50	N	30	S	37	Y	12	B
76	I	28	C	33	J	78	N	51	K	38	X	42	W	88	I	83	Z	6	I
32	H	70	M	2	C	70	I	23	R	4	F	72	M	15	Q	5	G	38	E
44	B	33	A	11	I	19	U	24	B	52	Q	58	E	8	N	59	M	Finish 86	F
62	D	48	W	20	W	10	O	18	D	85	W	54	J	64	T	31	H	84	P
90	E	47	W	36	L	25	X	99	V	96	U	66	Z	63	R	3	I	50	L
100	L	25	G	86	O	82	P	80	L	7	A	23	C	75	E	26	O	37	S

1. 22
2. 20
3. 16
4. 30
5. 45
6. 12
7. 38
8. 44
9. 59
10. 10
11. 18
12. 26

"Stick with me and we will go places!"

Solve for *n* 1 (Page 150)

1	2	3	4	5	6	7	8	9	10
11	12	13	14	15	16	17	18	19	20
21	22	23	24	25	26	27	28	29	30
31	32	33	34	35	36	37	38	39	40
41	42	43	44	45	46	47	48	49	50
51	52	53	54	55	56	57	58	59	60
61	62	63	64	65	66	67	68	69	70
71	72	73	74	75	76	77	78	79	80
81	82	83	84	85	86	87	88	89	90
91	92	93	94	95	96	97	98	99	100
A	B	C	D	E	F	G	H	I	J

Equations will vary.

Solve for *n* 2 (Page 155)

25	9	28	32	15	12	11	51	80	54
44	22	20	3	56	63	10	8	14	55
49	45	33	100	6	99	38	24	48	77
36	5	88	50	16	21	7	4	2	97
A	B	C	D	E	F	G	H	I	J

Equations will vary.

Solve for *n* 3 (Page 160)

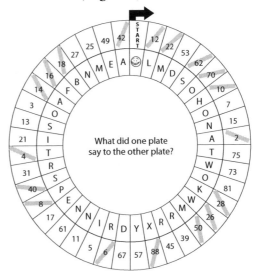

"Don't worry. Dinner is on me!"

Geometry (Page 165)

L trapezoid	M 13 inches	I obtuse angle	T perimeter
R symmetrical	E 3.5 inches	S 7.25 inches	I 7.5 inches
B less than 90 degrees	H more than 90 degrees	N line	S parallel lines
N five	A 7 inches	C 10.5 inches	R 6.5 inches
Finish four	M octagon	Y 4.5 centimeters	I horizontal
O hexagon	S 6 centimeters	U vertical	T 180°
M pentagon	E diameter	A horizontal	N 90°
A right angle	R radius	C trapezoid	U right angle
T line	I scalene triangle	O parallelogram	T isosceles triangle
E 15 inches	A symmetrical	N area	E quadrilateral
P intersecting lines	L parallel lines	A acute angle	R equilateral triangle
W obtuse angle	I right angle	M congruent	T sphere
G octagon	C angle	R perpendicular lines	K triangle
Start*	B ray	L parallelogram	E hexagon

It is an acute angle.

1. Students may draw any angle less than 90°.

2. Students should draw an obtuse angle (greater than 90°) and a right angle (exactly 90°).

Money (Page 170)

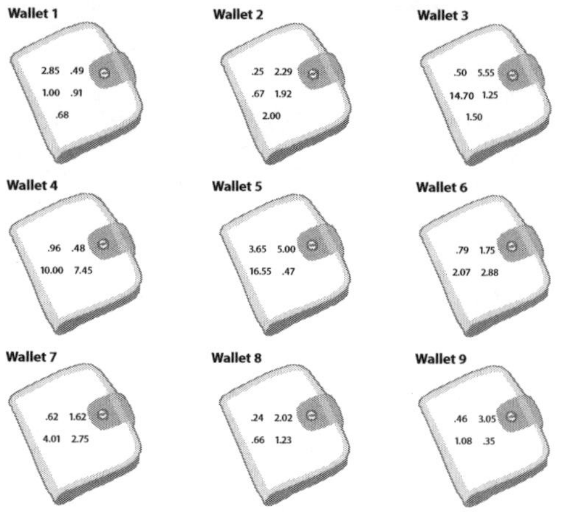
Wallet 1
2.85 .49
1.00 .91
.68
Wallet 2
.25 2.29
.67 1.92
2.00
Wallet 3
.50 5.55
14.70 1.25
1.50
Wallet 4
.96 .48
10.00 7.45
Wallet 5
3.65 5.00
16.55 .47
Wallet 6
.79 1.75
2.07 2.88
Wallet 7
.62 1.62
4.01 2.75
Wallet 8
.24 2.02
.66 1.23
Wallet 9
.46 3.05
1.08 .35

1. Wallet 5
2. Wallet 8
3. $9.68
4. $16.00

Time (Page 175)

Blue →	4:30	7:15	3:45	3:15	2:15	9:00	12:15	12:00	4:15	9:30
Red	6:15	11:00	11:30	10:15	7:00	8:30	1:30	11:15	10:00	1:45
Green	5:15	6:45	10:45	9:15	11:45	12:30	1:15	2:30	3:30	5:45
Orange	6:30	7:30	4:45	2:45	8:00	5:00	6:00	7:45	8:15	3:15

Blue (a.m.)	Green (p.m.)	Difference in Time
4:30	5:15	45 min
7:15	6:45	11 hrs 30 min
3:45	10:45	7 hrs
3:15	9:15	6 hrs
2:15	11:45	9 hrs 30 mins
9:00	12:30	3 hrs 30 min
12:15	1:15	1 hr
12:00	2:30	2 hrs 30 min
4:15	3:30	11 hrs 15 min
9:30	5:45	8 hrs 15 min

Measurement (Page 180)

12 centimeters	**Start** *	6 feet	80 ounces	46 inches	32 feet
15 quarts	16 square inches	9 gallons	11 years	10 hours	64 square inches
6 pints	18 inches	81 square inches	7 quarts	90 minutes	96 inches
20 quarts	24 cups	18 feet	2 inches	100 kilometers	88 cups
36 inches	32 ounces	8 tons	3 years	1 meter	60 quarts
54 square inches	5 inches	4 hours	2 miles	14 inches	40 inches
22 feet	48 eggs	38 inches	72 inches	18 eggs	66 cups
5 gallons	16 centimeters	4 square inches	49 square inches	32 centimeters	**Finish** 25 square inches
84 eggs	28 pints	48 quarts	12 yards	22 square inches	20 centimeters

Drawings will vary.

Probability (Page 185)

1/7 Z	1/6 A	5/12 F	7/8 H	Spinner 1 I	2/3 O	Bag 3 G
2/3 S	1/3 M	2/6 or 1/3 E	3/5 B	Spinner 6 C	3/5 E	**Finish** Spinner 7
4/10 or 2/5 K	Spinner 3 M	2/10 or 1/5 E	5/7 C	Spinner 9 C	2/7 A	green D
Bag 1 U	3/4 S	Bag 3 S	4/9 E	6/8 or 3/4 R	1/9 P	Card Set 2 I
5/7 E	2/5 P	3/12 or 1/4 T	Bag 4 P	2/12 or 1/6 B	Spinner 2 Y	Bag 1 Z
red O	4/8 or 1/2 A	Bag 2 B	3/4 E	9/12 or 3/4 S	1/10 R	5/6 R
blue T	purple M	Spinner 5 A	1/4 K	3/8 E	Spinner 4 S	2/3 T
7/12 Z	6/7 O	5/8 F	2/8 or 1/4 F	3/4 N	1/8 D	3/8 I
Spinner 2 H	1/5 E	Bag 1 M	3/5 S	Bag 7 N	4/9 E	1/4 I
Bag 2 E	3/8 Z	Spinner 7 E	**Start** *	2/4 or 1/2 R	0 S	3/6 or 1/2 M

Because pepper makes them sneeze

Spinners will vary.

All Possible Outcomes (Page 191)

1	2	3	4	5	6	7	8	9	10
11	12	13	14	15	16	17	18	19	20
21	22	23	24	25	26	27	28	29	30
31	32	33	34	35	36	37	38	39	40
41	42	43	44	45	46	47	48	49	50
51	52	53	54	55	56	57	58	59	60
61	62	63	64	65	66	67	68	69	70
71	72	73	74	75	76	77	78	79	80
81	82	83	84	85	86	87	88	89	90
91	92	93	94	95	96	97	98	99	100

Answers will vary but should include a tree diagram of a number that is highlighted in the table.

Data Analysis (Page 196)

Start *	bar graph	line graph	nature
organized table	438	organized tables	adventure
tally chart	about 52 degrees	about 89 degrees	34
ice-cream sundaes	biography	cookies and brownies	Mrs. Guzman
about 37 degrees	24	brownies and pie	30
June 5th and 8th	biographies and adventures	line graph	ice-cream sundaes and cookies
June 3rd	312	Data Set 5	Data Set 2
75	222	Data Set 3	300
Room 11	Room 12	9	137
Week 3	50 degrees	Week 4	10
7	52	75	**Finish** 371
2	12	adventure and nature books	200
about 18 degrees	biographies and nature books	43	nature books
20	pie and fruit	146	150

Answers will vary.

Notes

Notes

DATE DUE

			PRINTED IN U.S.A.